Who Am I, Really?

A textbook for the most illusive subject; yourself.

By: Cliff Said

Copyright© 2009 by Hoyt Opportunities LLC.
All Rights Reserved.

ISBN 978-0-9829530-0-6

Published by Impact Media division of

Hoyt Opportunities LLC.
1102 Grant Street
Scranton IA, 51462-0157

Hoyt Opportunities and Impact Media Logo(s) produced by Rob A. Hoyt

No part of this publication may be reproduced, stored, transmitted in any form or by any means except as permitted under Section 107 or Section 108 of the 1976 United States Copyright Act, without prior written permission from the publisher. Requests to the publisher for permission should be addressed to the Book Department, Impact Media 1102 Grant Street, Scranton, IA 51462-0157.

Limit of Liability; Disclaimer: The content of this book is meant to inspire and entertain the reader and was created and edited to the best of the ability of those involved with the project, but no warranty relative to the accuracy or completeness of the content, expressed or implied, Neither the publisher nor the author shall be held liable for any loss of profit or damages sustained through the reading of this book.

– Dedicated To –

My Wife Millie, without you I would be nothing. You are the core of my dedication and the daily inspiration to all that I do.

God truly sent you to me and I cherish every moment we have together.

You have such a deep abiding faith and your life constantly proves this. What an inspiration you have been to me for these fifty-one years. Honey, you are the wind beneath my wings. I truly love you!

Cliff

As I look back on my life there are so many people I need to thank for having patience and faith in me.

Miss Buddin was my High School English, Drama and Speech Teacher. Even though she struck fear in the hearts of most students, myself included, she taught me so much that I use today. She taught me that there are no limits only self-imposed limitations.

Mr. and Mrs. McDonald were my Music Teachers. Mr. McDonald taught instrumental music and Mrs. McDonald taught voice. Both of these people were a great influence on me. They encouraged me to do my best and it always paid off.

Dr. Dick Glasgow my pastor and dear friend. Even though Dick has moved on he continues to be not only my friend but my confidant. I can be totally open and vulnerable with him and he always supports me. His deep abiding faith and the way he lives his life is a constant inspiration to me. Thanks for your direction and for keeping me accountable.

Pastor Gordon Moen What a great friend he has become. His knowledge of the world and his ability to fuse it into what God has for him is a great inspiration and example. He is the epitome of knowing Who he is because he first knows Whose he is.

Darwin Hammer a great friend. Darwin was one of those once in a lifetime friends. He always allowed me to be who I was and encouraged me to be even more. He was constantly putting me in front of people who he thought could benefit from the experience and I always received the most. I know he is with God and that is comforting. I really miss you friend.

Senator Gary Dahl has gone from being a client to becoming one of my very best friends. Gary has enjoyed a tremendous amount of success in his life and is willing to share the excitement. Gary and his wife Deb are one's whom I have developed a strong covenant relationship with. Thanks for being who you are!

My Dad always included me in his projects. He was a great teacher and expressed his love in so many ways. The life lessons he taught me will never leave me. Integrity and sticking with a commitment was just a couple of those life lessons. I miss you dad!

My Mom showed her emotion easily and gave me the OK to do the same.

Her undying devotion to supporting her children was such a great example for us to raise our children. Mom, thanks for your approval and I really miss you.

Beverly Hoyt my sister, keeps me accountable and encourages me to stretch my faith and share it with others. She is truly an Angel! Love you sis!

Shirley Hoyt my sister, has been my sidekick from the get go. Thanks for always being there and for taking the heat for at least half of the trouble we got into as kids. You continue to provide a source of encouragement. Love you sis!

My Daughter Cindy has such a neat way of sharing her love. God has spoken and she has listened! Thanks for always being there to support me and for encouraging me to write this book.

My Daughter Tammy has such a strong faith. Her steadfast devotion to the Lord and her family is a source of real joy and inspiration. She is very emotionally attached to what God has called her to do. She is very drawn by the power of the Holy Spirit. Thank you for inspiring me to continue in the tough times and the good times.

My Son-in-Law David has a deep faith and his total concern for the welfare of this family is simply awesome. He has a very strong understanding of computers and this is a great benefit for me. Thank you for your steadfastness.

My Grand Son-in-Law J.B. Hinote I could not have chosen a better man to be the husband of my Grand Daughter and father of my Great Grand Children. He has a super deep faith and lives his life accordingly. What a Blessing.

My Grand Children – Lorelle, Anna, and Josef and my Great Grand Children Isaiah David, Lily Rayann, and Malachi James WOW! What can I say other then you are so great. Just talking with and seeing you inspires me to keep sharing. I love each of you for who you are and for who you will become!

Cliff Said...... What can I possibly say in the forward of this great book to relate to all the experiences I have had with Cliff over the years both personal and business?

My goal in life had always been to make it to retirement and have a few good years before the end. Then in 1985 I found myself out of work. At that point having no business experience I started a trucking company. With hard work and perseverance that business has today grown into a multimillion dollar a year business that is now owned by the employees. I am still involved and have also warehousing and distribution companies. Oh, I'm also an Illinois State Senator representing the 38th district in Illinois.

I first met Cliff in the early 90's while he was working for a neighboring business. We met and had some discussions about business and life in general. I scheduled Cliff to do a full company presentation on a Saturday. It was a huge success! That was the beginning of what was to become a long relationship {both personal and business} with Cliff and his wife Millie.

There are so many things in life that we all know we should do or not do. That pertains to business as well as personal and sometimes we need someone to help us see the big picture. Cliff is an expert at that, as this book will reveal. Every one will not get that same lesson from each page but every one will get the mental stimulation to start the mind working.

In most instances either business or personal the greatest enemy we have every day is the one we look at in the mirror each morning. This book takes us past that and gives insight as to how to move forward.

Enjoy and keep this book close for inspiration and information as your life goes forward.

Gary Dahl
Illinois State Senator

Chapter 1

Discovering the Inside You!

To begin the journey of looking inside we must first realize the need to do so. All quality committed action is first born within ourselves.

Ask yourself the following six questions to determine if you are ready for the journey.

1. As of late, are the results of my actions dependent on the input of others?

2. Am I confused about my direction more often?

3. Am I finding the results of my actions less important?

4. Is it just easier to go with the flow?

5. Am I happy in this obvious comfort zone?

6. Am I wanting to quit and not caring if I do?

Since you have probably answered yes to some of the above questions, you need to ask yourself one more question to unlock the door and start the journey.

Question: "Are you ready to take responsibility and ownership in creating the process of exchange in your life?" If your answer is yes, then proceed on and have a great trip.

To prepare yourself for this trip, you must do some specific things.

1. Find a quiet time and place to meditate in order to cleanse your mind of any clutter that might be present.

2. You must be willing to take the time to do the exercises. This book was not meant to be read in a hurry and then put away.

Now that you have done all of the above you are ready to begin.

First, I encourage you to look at life as a full-blown play with you as its star performer. This play goes on all your waking hours, every day, for all of your life. Pretty awesome isn't it! Most of us would rather other people or things take the responsibility for the negative experiences and we want full responsibility for the positive. If you are getting great or poor reviews to your play you must take the ownership for it. In other words, "If It Is To Be It Is Up To Me." These ten little two letter words when spoken with conviction bring us to the starting line and with God's help we will be energized.

All of our lives (plays) have a multifaceted story line - Comedy, Melodrama, Tragedy, Sit Com, and etc. There is a story that exemplifies this point very well.

There was a man who was born into a family willing to live a middle class existence. He decided early on that he did not want to live like this the rest of his life. So, he took action. Every night before he went to bed he got on his knees and prayed this prayer, "Dear God, please let me win the lottery." He did this every night for all of his life. Finally, reaching the later years of living and feeling that time had passed him by and that God had not listened, he prayed the following prayer, "God, I have been praying to you for 60 years asking you to please let me win the lottery. Why haven't you answered me?" With that, a loud booming voice came from above and said, "John, buy a ticket!"

This story, all to often defines the way we approach life. We start out with great intentions of setting the world on fire! Soon we find it very difficult. Greatness is a condition created within us and should not be measured by how terrific we are but rather by the positive support we lend to others and specific situations.

The biggest erosion to inner control is losing sight of the original dream. If this has happened to you, do not be discouraged for you are in the majority rather than the minority. The secret here is to do something about it. Age has no bearing here.

Several years ago, I was about to start a three-night class on "Personal Development Through Self Motivation" and was standing at the registration table. The time to start was at hand when gentlemen came in wanting to attend the session. The sign in people quickly signed him in and collected his fee. He apologized for being late but explained that he had just left his daughter and family who were helping him celebrate his eightieth birthday.

At the first break, I could not resist going to him and asking the obvious question, "What was an eighty year old man doing at a "Personal Development Through Self Motivation Seminar", and especially on his Birthday?" He answered me simply, "Because I'm not dead!"

He went on to say that every day he intended to learn something about himself, embrace it, glean from it, experience it and share it. You can imagine how encouraged and exhilarated I was about the work I was doing. George was positive proof that what I was teaching works. Just by being there and sharing himself, he touched the whole class and myself and moved us to a higher level.

I am sure some of you are saying that George probably had a very successful life and, therefore, it was easier for him to act that way. I am not sure if that is true or not. I am sure though that it makes no difference. I have spoken with people who have had tragedy be the basic way their lives were lived and they have that same quality attitude.

- Discover *Who* You Are -

*If you are a Lion make sure you are not trying
to be an elephant!*

What I want you to realize, is that where you are in your life right now has been determined by a number of choices you have made for a long time. I am sure you have all heard the statement, "Don't worry about where you are, there is always someone less fortunate than you." You know, "I worried about not having any shoes until I saw someone with no feet"! This is all well and good but when your feet are freezing, shoes are necessary! What I am really saying is, "Positive change/exchange can not be solely created by guilt"!

Guilt may be a wake up call, but positive change must be fueled by a burning inner desire to do so. This burning desire must be tied to an expected positive reward. This reward must become an acknowledged vision/dream. The vision/dream must be shared with all those around us, for only when we share it, will it reach its maximum potential.

As we continue this journey, I will line out a step-by-step program that will bring you the success you so richly deserve. Remember, age is not a factor.

Take at least one hour to complete

Find a quiet spot where you will not be interrupted and search inside of yourself for all the good qualities and, talents you have.

If you are having trouble thinking of some, take the time to ask a spouse or friend for suggestions.

This will trigger your inner self to continue. Most of us have trouble tooting our own horn.

Just remember this is an awareness tool for your eyes only. Write as many as you can think of on your positive page.

As you continue on with this book, you will think of more to add to your list. Be sure to go back and add them.

This should be an exhilarating experience providing you with the euphoric feeling of a standing ovation.

It is OK to feel good and to say I am pretty terrific.

Now use the same procedure to identify the negative aspects of the inner you. List these on the page following your positive qualities. This will not be as much fun but is very necessary in building your foundation of change.

Now, on a separate sheet of paper take each quality/talent you have identified and write a brief accounting of when you have used it and what the results were. These can either be recent or out of your past. Take your time!

Now, do the same exercise with the negative aspects of your inner self.

When you have completed this step/procedure go back to what you have written about each element and determine what more you could have done to increase the positive results and what you could have done differently to change the negative results. Write these down!

Pretty amazing isn't it! You have just taken the first and most vital step in creating positive change in your life. It never ceases to amaze me the number of people I work with in my Workshops who have never taken the time to discover themselves.

There is an old saying that applies here, "If you keep doing the same thing you will continue getting the same results!" Another potent statement which applies here comes from my twelve-step program. "Insanity is continuing the same behavior and expecting a different result!"

When I first completed this exercise I was appalled to discover the number of times I was using my negative side and was lulled into thinking it was positive.

Now that you have made the decision to start and have done the beginning exercises, next lets talk about what to do with the information. You know that information is data crunched down into a usable form. Judith Sills in her book, "Excess Baggage," expresses the need for us to know that our strengths are also our weaknesses. I couldn't agree more. I mention this so that you will be prepared to put in the safeguards that will keep your ship in balance.

"You have four seconds to impress or depress even yourself!"

The Morning and a New Beginning!

A beginning is so important and every day is your opportunity to begin.

Let me share with you seven exercises to begin your day. These will help insure you a positive experience. Remember, I said insure you a positive experience not irradiate your stress!

Before you start though I must ask you a very important question.

"Have you ever been accused of being strange and crazy"?

If the answer is yes this exercise will seem valid and supportive. If the answer is no then you need to make a special effort to engage in the following exercise. A key ingredient to this exercise is what I have done the night before.

I take about fifteen to thirty minutes per night to journal my day. I journal all the positive experiences I have had, the people who have made a difference, and the one's I have had the opportunity to make a difference to.

Step 1:

Wake up! Seems simple, but there are no guarantees. Having just recently experienced a major heart attack and open-heart surgery, I have developed a much keener respect for just waking up! Take the time to say thank you for waking up and for the privilege of seeing the day. George Burns said, "When I get up, I read the obituary column and if my name is not in there, I know I'm still in the game!" Not a bad approach. I put my feet on the floor and start to sing. (Zipity do dah) Then I say "Thank you God for this beautiful day and for my chance to share it."

Step 2:

Go into the bathroom, look at yourself in the mirror, and say out loud, "You are terrific and every day you get better and better." I know you think this is very close to being quite egotistical. Well it is. Let me share with you, there is a very fine line between self-esteem and egotism. Your friends, fellow workers, and most assuredly your relatives will be glad to tell you when you cross over the line. Go for it! When you toot your own horn it prepares you to be the best you can be and makes you ready to serve.

Step 3:

If you can't sing while setting on the edge of the bed, then try singing in the shower! If you don't want to do that because you can't sing, remember, the shower doesn't care! If only the birds that could sing well sang, the woods would be a quiet place. Isn't it interesting that even when the birds are singing in the cracks it sounds beautiful and relaxing? The importance of this exercise is to get all things working in sync.

Step 4:

This is a very important step and will provide, for you, the most power to achieve. Go to all the people in your house and tell them how much you appreciate their presence. You might try saying "I Love You" and mean it. If you are living alone, then call somebody if possible or find someone as soon as you can to do this. The reason most people do not do this on a regular basis is because we are caught up in the process of making a living instead of making a life. You see, this step, will fill you with warmth, strength, peace, and hope for it is impossible to give a hug without receiving one.

> Note: Hugs are not always physical; most of us are starving for hugs, the positive reinforcement to our worth. This particular exercise is as important at the end of the day as it is at the beginning of the day. At the end of the day it serves as proof of your integrity and commitment.

I remember many years ago when I was traveling on the road selling floor covering. I typically left on Monday and returned on Friday. On this particular Friday, after a very difficult week as I returned home my three-year-old Granddaughter was waiting for me. She and I had a special bond.

She had taken her chair and set it on the deck of our house so she could see me come in the driveway. Now remember, I was absolutely beat and was looking forward to getting home and just relaxing. I pulled into my driveway and immediately noticed my granddaughter who was by now jumping up and down hollering, "Grandpa! Grandpa"! I was glad to see her but I would have to admit I was wishing she had come over later after I had some time to regroup.

I stopped my vehicle and was getting out when she could not wait any longer. It was summer time and she was barefoot but you see she was a little different than most kids. She did not like to walk or run through the grass barefoot. However her desire to see Grandpa over-rode her dislike of running barefoot in the grass. I was greeted with her hollering, "ouch - ouch - ouch!" as she ran towards me.

When she got to me she reached up and grabbed my tie, swung up into my arms, threw her arms around my neck, gave me a big hug, and a kiss and said, "Grandpa, I really love you"! Needless to say my tired and aching body was instantly revived.

By this time her mother and grandmother were out on the deck to see what was happening. Her grandmother said to her, "ask him to take you to Paris"! Of course this was to say I was willing to do anything for her because she had touched my most vulnerable emotion deep in my heart.

Today she is twenty-six years old and can still create that positive energy flow in me.

Step 5:

Get up fifteen to thirty minutes earlier than what you normally do. (I know this is an awesome task but try it you might find it to be very beneficial) Find a special spot where you can be alone and won't be interrupted. This is the time I spend in quality meditation with God, asking for direction and making myself available to His will. I study the word to confirm what I hear God directing me to do. Take a look at the day ahead of you. Try to visualize your day in one or two hour blocks of time. Have your daily planner in front of you and line out your expectations of the day. Be sure and leave flexible time for the unexpected. I then read my journal from the previous day. This empowers me to be immediately prepared to meet the day's expectations.

Step 6:

This step is a lot of fun and is meant to stimulate your creative juices as well as become contagious for others. As you are leaving for work and you are starting your car, I want you to start to laugh. Now then I don't mean a weak ha - ha. I mean reach down inside you and really laugh. If you are concerned about what to laugh at, do what I do, pull the mirror down. It works for me and I bet it will work for you. It would be good if you did this all the way to work.

I know you are afraid someone will see you laughing all by yourself and you are concerned about what they will think. If you worry about what people think of you, if you knew how little they did, you would not worry. Besides, you are just giving them positive reinforcement to what they have thought about you for a long time - You are Strange and Crazy!

If you have not been accused of being strange and crazy, then you have chosen to just accept what is going on in your life and are expecting to have the same or worse everyday.

Step 7:

As you are driving to work seek out someone who is obviously in the mood of "I owe – I owe – so off to work I go" and make an effort to wave and smile at them. If you live in a big city then use common sense and don't incite road rage. However, you may find this to be very empowering to you as well.

Just the other day I saw this person stopped at the stoplight going the opposite direction of me. He was definitely in the afore mentioned mood or worse. As we passed by each other I waved and smiled. He almost broke his neck trying to see who I was. I decided to go around the block and catch him at the next stoplight and repeat my effort. I know he went to work and asked if anybody knew someone from Iowa with P.M.A. on his license plate. And I am sure he expressed his concern about the sanity of this person. However, you must realize this made him concentrate on something and someone else besides himself. Mission accomplished!

These exercises will take very little of your precious time in the morning, yet it will have a major impact on your time management and attitude for the rest of the day.

Attitude is the Key!

There are four types of people: Cling-on's, Spectators, Participants and Investors. Cling-on's are those who just hang around in hopes somebody will make it happen for them. Spectators are the ones who just want to watch others do it and steal the thunder when it happens. Participants are the ones who will get involved as long as they are told what to do and then they only go to that level. Investors are those who see not only the big picture but also are able stay focused on the present. Investors always go the extra mile and are richly rewarded for it. Besides, the extra mile has no traffic jams! If you have heard yourself say recently, "Someday I'll do that" you will eventually retire and say "I could have if only". All the reasons we use not to take action now will continue to cause negative results.

There is a great old saying which plays true for all of us: "I have met the enemy and he is me!" We then engage in negative self-talk… "I just don't have time right now." This is to say, someday I will. We must quit kidding ourselves and realize there are some things we just aren't going to do. We need to program ourselves daily to achieve the things that are important to us and our committed life with others.

Important is the operative word here. Unfortunately, we too often spend all our time on urgent things. This is not to say our lives are not impacted by urgency. It would be infinitely better though if we would organize our day factoring in those things that are important, tying a sense of urgency to them which will insure our commitment and leaving flexible time to deal with the unexpected urgencies. This is all about becoming a meaningful specific instead of a wandering generality. (See step #5 in the previous chapter)

Now let me talk about some things that will get in your way and send your ship off course. If you are going to stay on course, you need to be aware of as many of the potholes as possible. There will be enough unexpected ones as it is. Being aware will help you keep your train on track and off the dirt road.

Carry over! Things and attitudes of yesterday not being dealt with and brought into the next day.

Letting the lack of planning on the part of others to create an emergency on your part.

Not having specific daily, weekly, monthly, yearly, and lifetime goals tied to our vision.

Low self esteem caused by age, gender, appearance, failure, stress and etc.

Bitterness caused by your unwillingness to forgive.

Now lets take a look at each of these and see what creates them and discover what we can do to combat them. If you are feeling any of these you can't ignore them. If someone says to you that you should not feel that way, remember you do.

Carry over we simply did not get everything done today so we carry it over to tomorrow. At the end of your day, take some special time to analyze what is left. There will be some things that need to be carried over and some things that need to be discarded for now or even forever. The things that need to be carried over, factor them into the next days time. Do not allow this action to cause you stress because you had to put something off until tomorrow.

Remember; always plan according to the level of importance. Develop the attitude that it is acceptable to have things left over as long as you re-evaluate its level of importance. Most of us waste a lot of precious time agonizing over what we didn't get done. This is self-defeating and will eventually cause you to be a wandering generality. If you have ever had trouble sleeping at night because you can't shut your mind off it is more than likely caused by carry over. The following exercise will help you get past this dilemma.

When you lay down in bed bring the things you are thinking about up on your minds computer screen one at a time. Once you have concentrated on just one then mentally transfer it across the room and put it on a shelf promising yourself that you will pick it up in the morning. Continue this exercise until all the subjects have been removed and are on the shelf for the morning. This is not an easy exercise to do but with some practice it will work. If you get five hours of unencumbered sleep it will give you more energy than ten hours of restless sleep.

I know you have all experienced waking up in the morning more tired than when you went to bed. An interesting side note: Most of the things you put on the shelf, when you appraise them in the morning you will find they weren't worthy of any effort in the first place and therefore can be deleted from your memory bank.

Others lack of planning; we must take control here. It is our decision as to what part of others needs we are going to support. I believe we need to support others by being involved in their process. However, we are not doing them any favor if we continually allow their unorganized efforts to negatively impact our lives.

This is the time for you to become assertive and help them to become organized. Show them the process of planning their life and how these planned expectations will reward them. Do not be discouraged if you find that one person who delights in being a wandering generality. It is your responsibilities to let that go and move on.

DO NOT try to fix them. They really do not want to be fixed. There is a saying that applies here, "There are two things you need to know; There is a God and You aren't him!"

It is important here to share with the one who is unorganized that you can't operate in that arena and if the project is a joint one they will have to follow the organized plan. Make sure you realize though, if the project is all theirs then leave them alone and let them do as they wish.

No Vision or Goals this is like having no rudder on your ship. No values, no direction, no vision, no hope. This is a true wandering generality. We will address the goal setting process completely in another chapter.

Low Self Esteem this a condition that, with some, seems constant and with others is a come and go thing. There are many causes to low self-esteem.

One primary cause is feeling less than adequate for the task. Our inadequacy is created in our mind by many things. Some real and some perceived. For example, knowing we are less educated on the subject than others is very real, but feeling others are better than us is perceived. However, it makes no difference what the cause, the feeling is very real. Being less knowledgeable about something can provide an opportunity to learn. Remember the story of George who at 80 came to learn. It is never too late to gain insight and knowledge.

The feeling of inferiority is a common one and is difficult to deal with. I can only suggest that you go back through the daily wake up exercise and listen to the value of it. There is a powerful message that applies here, "Your OK! Because God don't make no junk!" Specifically remember the second step in the wake up preparation for your day. You might add to that statement this,"I will always be a second best somebody else but I am the very best me there is!"

Being the best you and pushing yourself to the edge of being better everyday will provide for you a tremendous foundation of positive self-esteem. Self-esteem will be built by becoming wise, but pay special care to the idea that knowledge is not wisdom.

There will always be someone more knowledgeable than you. Wisdom is the ability of knowing the value of the knowledge and then being able to impart it to others.

Self-esteem is an internal thing and requires constant self-talk and a solid belief that you are important. Some people suffer with low self-esteem because they have never been approved of. Just remember, motivation is a personal thing and inspiration is a shared thing. When searching back in their life we find that their parents did not give them the approval or support and their peers did not either. This is a tough situation to get past. However, you must begin by realizing that saying "I love you" begins with yourself.

Happiness is a matter of choice. The difficult part of searching for approval is that the harder we try and get it the more illusive it becomes. The secret here is to let all those around you know that you are okay with yourself and then lighten up on the effort to get others to say it. You see when you are pushing for it others see you as self centered and obnoxious and they turn you off. The operative situation here is to like yourself, let others know that you like and appreciate them, and the support, feelings, and values will return to you many times over. Also remember that not everybody will think you are greater than sliced bread. You need to be okay with that also.

The most important thing here is to make the decision that you want things to be different from this moment on - then create that by investing yourself in the above process. Stop bringing up past failures and feelings. Surround yourself with those people who you support and those that support you.

I might add that if your heart is aching and hardened or if you seem to be defensive all the time to others and their actions towards you then you may need to develop some calluses on your knees. There is tremendous power in prayer and getting in touch with your spiritual side.

Some forty-eight years ago when I first got into the work world I began as a salesman for a furniture store. The man that owned the store had only an eighth grade education. That being said he was one of the wisest men I have ever known. He did not let education or the lack of knowledge stand in his way. He developed a tremendous thirst, hunger and passion for success.

He discovered early on that people were his greatest commodity and so he became very wise in dealing with people. Today I credit him for my solid foundation of "People Skills" and for showing me that I was the main reason for my success or failure. His favorite statement was "others and things can slow you down but only you can stop yourself completely!" Lack of self-esteem is a major roadblock and will bring your train to a grinding stop!

The Art of Forgiveness

Unwillingness to forgive; The action of forgiving is one of the most energy giving things you can do. By the way, it is also one of the most difficult. Bare this directive in mind, forgiving is the action, not forgetting. When someone does something to us that we feel is unfair, in order for us to be free of the burden, we must follow three basic levels of forgiveness:

Forgive others; Forgiving the one or ones who you feel did you wrong will be tough, but if you don't you are the only loser. The one or ones that might have caused your angst are not feeling the pain. This is an action that must take place. The most productive way to achieve this is to search out the person or persons and tell them how you feel and forgive them for their action. You must be prepared for them to deny their involvement. It is acceptable for them to do that. It is not acceptable for you to shut them down because of it. We must keep in mind that our purpose is to rid ourselves of the energy draining poison we are carrying. We can only hope they want to do the same. If they tell you to drop dead, then just say "Thank You" and move on. This in itself will make them aware that you are serious and wish to get past it. When we carry bitterness with us it is like drinking a glass of poison and expecting the other person to die.

Forgiving God is very important; We all have a tendency that when things go wrong for quite a while to say, "Why me

God?" "What Have I done to deserve this?" Of course, we all know that God didn't look down and say, "I think I will get you today." God is very loving and forgiving. It is important for us to realize that He has forgiven us before we can even feel guilty. God does not carry a grudge. God does not get upset because we blame him he just makes it clear for us to see our direction. When we open our eyes and pay attention, He will provide us with the vision and strength to face and deal positively with any situation. We must remember that He provides for us a way but we must take the action. A good friend of mine shared an experience he had one time in the middle of the night. It seems he kept waking up and trying to deal with a certain issue. He finally decided to get up and go out to his den and read the word and pray. He felt God telling him this – "Yes it has happened. Now let me help you." This is a very powerful message and by the way, He will help you every time!

Forgiving yourself; When we really feel guilty about what action or lack of action we have taken, it is easy to blame ourselves and beat up on ourselves for it. Until you forgive yourself, you negate all the empowerment you have created by forgiving others and God. Remorse is awareness and a wake up tool but has very little positive energy connected to it. We all make mistakes. In fact, if I had my life to live over, I would make more mistakes, hopefully not the same ones.

This reminds me of the story about the Banker who had just retired and was being interviewed by a local news person. The Banker was asked to what he attributed his success He replied, "Making good decisions." to which the reporter responded, "How do you make good decisions?" The Banker replied, "Experience," The reporter asked, "How do you get experience?" The Banker answered," Making bad decisions." Making the decision to take action is infinitely more important than if it was a good or bad decision. You will not have the opportunity to run the race let alone win if you don't go to the starting line.

In order for this to work you must make it acceptable to make a bad decision. This is a mind set that takes time and effort to create. Try starting with the little decisions of your life. Become accustomed to making quick and well-founded decisions. Remember, if you make a bad decision, forgive yourself and make another decision using the knowledge you gained from the previous decision. Our lives are filled with choices and our destiny is in our hands. I challenge you to be responsive, take charge, and be an owner/investor.

When you don't forgive yourself you fall into the trap of being a
CLING – ON!

When I look at the word "FORGIVE," I see it as an action word. The following is a break down of each letter and how it impacts the end result.

F – Freedom The underlying motive for forgiveness is to be Free! This feeling of being free encompasses many aspects of our lives, including work relationships, as well as personal relationships.

O – Originate You must be the one to begin the process. We all have a tendency to have a wait and see attitude. The power you will create for yourself when you are the originator is unprecedented.

R – Relinquish You must develop the art of letting go of the original motive for not forgiving. This is very difficult because we must take a portion of the responsibility for it happening in the first place.

G – Grace There are two kinds of grace here. First, consider the power of God's Grace. When you tap into this, He will provide you with the insight and   strength to do what you alone could never do. Second, you must be willing to give a grace period to those you are forgiving. They may not be prepared to receive your action at the moment. They may not feel they have done anything to be forgiven for.

I – Invite This is the action of asking the one or ones you need to forgive to hear you. Again realize they may not want to listen at this time. Keep sending out the invitation and the possibility of a two-way positive experience will be there.

V – Verify This action is very necessary as the process unfolds. Its primary purpose is to keep you focused on why you need to forgive in the first place. Remember, verify your action not others.

E – Experience As you go through the action, embrace every moment of the situation. The true experience is not just you having done it, but rather the whole experience – physically, emotionally and spiritually. Hugs are very supportive to the process if they are given in genuine kindness with no strings attached. In fact you can hug someone without even touching him or her. This comes in the way you speak and your body language.

Forgiving will empower you to achieve things you never thought possible. It will not only show respect to others it will give you your portion also. When we carry the burden of not forgiving, it consumes our precious time and creates a negative drain on our energy. If you follow the above plan of forgiving you will find that you will file those burdens very deep in your memory and therefore forget them. I realize that forgetting is a horse of a different color however, it is possible to do so if you work on it. It may take some time depending on the situation and the other parties involved and there are also those people that do not want to forget or to let you forget. These people are "Toxic Personalities" and you need to remove yourself from them as much as possible. If you can't stay completely clear of them then develop a plan to ward off their caustic attitude.

The best plan I have found is to create a positive atmosphere by supporting their worth and reinforcing their abilities. One of two things will take place:

1. They will see the light and decide to exchange their negative way of living for a more positive way, the one demonstrated by you.

2. They will become very uncomfortable and remove themselves from the scene.

Of course you will strive for number one to take place. However, if number two is the action then do not take on any guilt for this. Some people cannot live without conflict in fact it is their source of energy. The sad part of this is that they are leaving a great deal of life lying in the field on the ground and there is no going back!

The other part of forgiving is when we need to be forgiven. The operative action here is for us to take the initiative to ask for forgiveness. Here again, we must be prepared for the person to not be able to forgive us at that time. The very best we can do is ask to be forgiven and honestly say we are sorry for our actions. You can still have that all needed feeling of being set free even when the one you are asking to forgive you will not.

This is achieved through a specific mind set which is, when you ask to be forgiven mentally, shed any guilt you have and make it acceptable for the person to receive it however they chose to receive it. The intended goal here is to let go of the self-imposed guilt you may be feeling. Remember, there are some people who are just waiting for you to offend them and they will be reluctant to forgive you. An interesting note here, is that whether you are needing to be forgiven or needing to forgive others the responsibility for initiating the action lies in your hands.

Let me share a very personal story and as much as it causes me pain I can now share it because I have been forgiven and have forgiven.

My oldest sister and I had for a great number of years had a problem with supporting each other. She felt I was leading a less than respectful life and I thought she was meddling. We chose to tolerate each other for many years. I know my mother suffered greatly because of this for her heart ached for us to be brother and sister again.

I can't even tell you what was the original cause of the differences and of course now that isn't important. The fact that I can't remember does exemplify the tragedy of the situation. This, "I'll tolerate and you'll tolerate me but lets not get to involved with each other" went on for over thirty years. It wasn't until after I had a major heart attack and open heart surgery that I realized how much I was missing. She was tremendous help to my wife and children during this crisis.

I finally came to my senses and had to take ownership for not doing what I was teaching others to do in my workshops. It still took me some time to decide that I needed to mend the fence and ask for forgiveness but by the Grace of God and much prayer I was able to go to her and initiate the action. This was one of the greatest days of my life.

We told each other that we were sorry that we had let this happen - we hugged, cried and became brother and sister for the first time in thirty five years! I share this story with you so that if you are suffering from something like this please don't wait, Do It Now! This is also a great example of what my friend heard from God:

OK, it has happened. Now let me help you!

The Power Source

The next step in this journey is defining your "Power Source." This is the center or nucleus of your whole being, physically, emotionally, and spiritually. Your "Power Source" is the center core of your life.

Most people have never taken the time to even realize they have a specific "Power Source" let alone discover what it is. You may be asking, " Why do I need to know about my "Power Source?" My answer is very simple, "It will determine the success or failure of any endeavor you set out to do."

To better explain this, it is like having a tool with one power source and many attachments. Once we have identified our basic Power Source we can start determining what attachments fit. Many times we fail to perform at a high level because we are using attachments that do not fit our "Power Source." This is not to say, we cannot redesign our unit to accept a new attachment. This is done through education and a desire to learn. It is, however, important for us to realize that there are attachments and tools available that will never fit our "Power Source." In other words, there are some things that we are just not called to do. Again the three sides of your Power Source are:

   1.) Physical - your strength to physically achieve

   2.) Emotional - attitude and determination

   3.) Spiritual - your connection to a higher power, God who gives you vision, hope and direction

To help you better understand the definition process, the following guidelines should help.

> A. Define what kind of person you are (leader, follower, helper, supporter, laid back and etc..
>
> B. What are the things you most like to get involved with? Write these down. You will be amazed on how they fit the kind of person you are.
>
> C. Determine how many of these you are experiencing in your every day life.

Discovering what kind of person you are will help you determine the tools or attachments that best fit your internal power unit. An example - If you are a leader, put yourself in a position to lead. Step forward, take charge of things and show your organizational skills.

You will know when you are using an attachment that does not fit for it will make you miserable. When it does not fit, make sure you have the burning desire to redesign your unit to make it fit. In other words, make sure you will invest yourself in the education process that it takes to make it a fine tuned tool. If you do not have the burning desire then let it go.

Our failure almost always comes when we attempt to do things we are not equipped to do. On the other hand, when we stay focused on our physical, emotional and spiritual Power Source, using the proper attachments we will almost never fail!

To better understand your base take a little time to do the following exercise.

VALUES APPRAISAL

On a scale of one through twenty indicate the relative importance of each of the listed categories as they apply to you:

MUSIC	_____	AUTHORITY	_____
VACATION	_____	AUTOMOBILE	_____
JEWELRY	_____	WARDROBE	_____
FRIENDS	_____	HOME (HOUSE)	_____
SPORTS	_____	CHARITY	_____
SERVICE	_____	HEALTH	_____
PATRIOTISM	_____	READING	_____
CAREER	_____	FAMILY	_____
INFLUENCE	_____	SEX	_____
THEATER	_____	RELIGION (FAITH)	_____

Remember, this exercise is meant to help you establish a pattern for your "Power Source" so be totally honest. If there are areas you feel you have too much priority on then make the decision to redirect your efforts. This is the act of making the tools fit the power source. The main thing here is to not agonize over what you wished was high on your list but rather develop a plan to create what you truly can be!"

Several years ago while I was directing a Workshop on "Personal Development Through Self Motivation" I had the participants do the this exercise.

When they had finished I asked them the following questions; How many of you put family in the top five. Almost all of them raised their hands. I then asked how many of you put health in the top five? Again many raised their hands. I asked how many of you put friends in the top five? Several raised their hands. I asked how many of you put religion in the top five? Quite a few hands went up again. I then asked how many of you put career in the top five? A few hands went up but not very many. I then asked the question where do you spend bulk of your awake productive time? They answered at work. I shared, if that is true and it isn't high on your priority list then that may be the reason for the mediocrity you may be experiencing. I further shared with them that if they did not have career high on the list then everything else would suffer including their health.

You see, when you are unhappy in your work then negative stress becomes a major factor and it will take its toll in every aspect of your life. You will find yourself looking for what is wrong in every situation. When you have a passion for what you do you will never "WORK" another day in your life and you will have a sense of peace in all that you do.

After this discussion I asked one more question. How many of you put "Sex" in the top six or seven? A few timid hands went up and snickering broke out in the room. I then shared with them that I was talking about the sex drive (emotion) not the actual sex act. I went on to explain that the sex drive we possess is the most powerful drive we have. It will never give up; it is creative, and always very cunning. I stated that the next time they have a very difficult task to do they should try transmuting some of that incredible sex drive into achieving it. It takes a little work but you can actually do this.

At the end of the class two young men came up to me and complained that I had embarrassed them. I asked, how did I embarrass you? They answered that they were setting next to two Catholic Nuns when I asked the sex question and that made them look for a hole to crawl into. I was searching for what I was going to say to appease their concern when I heard my name being called from behind me. I turned around to see who was calling and there stood the two Nuns.

One of them offered to help and I immediately accepted. This is what that most incredible Sister said; "When the other Sister and I made the decision to become totally committed to the Church do you think that God came down, unscrewed the top of our heads and removed our sex drive? Of course He did not do this. The fact Is, we have perfected the art of doing exactly what Cliff is talking about and believe me it does work!" They turned and started to walk away leaving us with our mouths hanging open when suddenly they turned around and said this; "That is why we hardly ever fail!"

What a profound positive statement and affirmation of what I was teaching. As an interesting side note, I have heard from those two young men off and on over the years that have past and they claim that it works better and better, as you are willing to buy into it and let it work. In addition one of the Nuns said that every day she would pray for me to continue sharing what God had lain upon my heart and inspiring people to be the best they can be. This has been several years ago and I know she is still praying.

We humans are a very complex machine with a very simple control panel. When we go astray, it is generally for two reasons:

    1.) We make it more difficult than it really is.

2.) We try and take total control instead of leaning on the one who made us.

When we want to strengthen ourselves physically, we get ourselves involved in a good exercise program and maintain a well balanced diet.

To get us strengthened emotionally, we instill a quality Positive Attitude, read supportive material, and surround ourselves with positive people.

Then to strengthen ourselves spiritually, we spend time meditating, reading the Bible and any other material that supports the belief in a higher power, and become active in groups that help us gain knowledge and wisdom in our belief.

You see there is really nothing difficult about this at all. We must be willing to get out of our own road. The power to change and exchange is given to us all, the difficult part is allowing it to take place mainly because we must stretch ourselves past our present comfort zone. We all want to feel comfortable and when we are we feel this equates to happiness. When one gets too comfortable they begin to stagnate and eventually begin to smell.

Just remember -

"Success is on the opposite side of Good Enough!"

Now stop reading and do the following exercise. When complete take considerable time to reflect on what you have learned so far. It is now that you should be searching for your inner purpose.

From the list circle the 10 Characteristics/Traits, which you think BEST DISTINGUISHES **YOU**

Then place an "X" to the left of the ONE characteristic or trait which you feel is most unique about you...

Use this to help discover your purpose and the depth of your resolve.

Adventuresome	Loyalty
Alert	Neatness
Attention to Details	Open-minded
Calmness	Optimistic
Candid	Orderly (likes routine)
Challenges- -Likes Them	Outgoing
Concentration	Patient (Patience)
Conversational	Persistent
Consistent	Playful (ness)
Cooperative	Poise
Creative	Polite (ness)
Curious	Punctuality
Dependable	Quiet
Determined	Responsible
Easygoing	Responsive to Others
Emotional Stability	Reserved
Empathetic	Risk - Taker
Endurance	Self - Confident
Enthusiastic	Self – Reliant
Expressive of Feelings	Sense of Humor
Firm (ness)	Sensitive
Healthy	Sincere
Imaginative	Spontaneous
Initiating Ideas & Actions	Strong (Under Stress)
Innovative	Sympathetic (Warm)
Insightful	Systematic
Flexible	Tactful
Generosity	Can think on my feet
Gets Along With Others	Thorough
Good Judgment	Tidy (Work Place)Tolerant
High Energy Level	Versatile
Honesty	Vigor
Likes People	

P - - - - PREPARE (Know your power sources)
- 1. Physical
- 2. Emotional
- 3 Spiritual

U - - - - UNDERSTAND (It is internal not external)
- 1. Seek
- 2. Discover
- 3. Evaluate

R - - - - REALITY (It is *you* not someone's idea of *you*)
- 1. Take the time to look inside yourself
- 2. Believe in yourself
- 3. Seek God's face to lead you

P - - - - PLAN (It is your responsibility to create)
- 1. Set aside the time to pray for guidance
- 2. Journal what has happened
- 3. Look at the models God provides

O - - - - OPPORTUNITY (Know that God has provided this for you)
- 1. Expect this at every turn
- 2. Seize it
- 3. Experience it, Taste it and believe it

S - - - - SINCERITY (Provides strength)
- 1. Internal confirmation of Whose and Who you are
- 2. Creates a bond with others
- 3. Keeps you accountable

E - - - - EXPECT (Creates a platform of probable success)
- 1. Keeps your vision on track
- 2. Keeps your attitude positive
- 3. Keeps you open to God's Blessings

Making Sense of What You Learned

In chapter one, when you completed the exercise of identifying your positive qualities and negative qualities, how did you feel? If you felt you were falling short of what you have the talent to do, the following information will help you get beyond that. If you feel you are doing pretty well in this area, this information will help you go to the next level.

First and foremost, we must realize that we will always have talents and capabilities that we don't use to there fullest potential. This is the human side of us. However, we can become totally disabled by negative self-talk. I am speaking of that inner voice which occasionally says, "You can't do that!" We can say that we will not listen to that voice but realistically we know there are times when we will let the voice win.

The real secret here is to minimize the number of times you let the voice win. One of the best ways to do this is to go back to chapter two, "The Morning and a New Beginning" and put into action the morning exercises we discussed. Just remember, when you say it can't be done there are others doing it. Nothing will strengthen your defense like a great offense. Of course, the reason for starting your day this way is to shore up your offense and to set a precedence of making negative action unacceptable.

When I am directing my seminars, I will ask, "How many of you are morning people? That is, who of you really enjoy getting up in the morning?" The response is generally pretty low. The majority of the people would enjoy sleeping in. I state that I am not going to try and make morning people out of them. However, I am going to give them a road map - a plan on how to start their day more positively. Then I share the "How to start your day" exercise.

The single most important part of this exercise is to take the time to quietly meditate alone and communicate with God so as to make sure your plan of expectations aligns with His. When you do this you increase your probable success ratio 100%.

Watch out for these roadblocks when you begin the "Start Your Day Exercise" :

First, not feeling we have the time. The secret here is to allocate the time and make it a habit.

Second, family seeing this as dumb and making us feel we have gone completely around the bend. The secret here is to show them the benefit of your actions and encourage them to follow suit.

Just remember, when you worry about what people think of you, you must understand how little they really do. In any case ask yourself this question: What I am doing now, how is that working for me? I am sure you will come to the decision that exchanging some of your ways will provide and opportunity for positive growth.

When we have gained knowledge and insight, it remains totally useless until we put it into action!

The next four chapters will be devoted to the action side of the knowledge you have gained about yourself.

Chapter 7

Responsibility

We have been hearing since we were very small children that we must take the responsibility for our actions. I totally agree with this value but also realize it has become so mundane in its use that it falls on deaf ears most of the time.

You see when we hear that statement "you must take the responsibility for what you have **or** have not done" our defenses immediately go up and we mentally, if not verbally, say - I AM taking the responsibility. But are we really, deep down inside, taking the responsibility?

When we do this, we know that excuses and reasons do not count, only results. We realize the typical human way to react is to find something or someone to transfer the responsibility to. It is our nature not to be accountable for failure. The interesting fact is that we will take immediate responsibility for any and all successes. I have known those who are so paranoid about responsibility that they miss getting the credit for their successes.

I remember that at the end of one of my seminars on Hospitality and Customer service one of the employees asked for some personal time with me. When we got together, his first statement to me was "I can tell you what is wrong with this company." I, of course, encouraged him to forge on. He said "they treat you like dirt around here". I asked, "how long have you worked here?" He said, " about 10 years." I proposed, "how long have they treated you like dirt?" He said, "for 10 years!" to which I responded, "it seems to me you must like the treatment!"

If we do not like what is going on in our lives, we are the ones who are responsible for creating change even if that change is moving on. I went on to explain to him that if we want to receive the rewards in our life we must also be willing to pay the price. This man clearly wanted someone else, namely the company, to be responsible for his personal happiness. If we follow that path, then we must accept what they dish out! My father, rest his soul, shared with me long ago that, "you are either part of the solution or you are part of the problem.

Response - ability dictates that you should *respond* to your ability **not** *react* to it. When you respond, it is always positive and when you react, it is always negative. Again, look back at the exercise, in Chapter two and you will see each of the steps is tied to creating, for you, a day filled with positive expectations and they will prepare you to take charge and make it happen. Lincoln put it best when he said, " folks can be about as happy as they chose to be!"

Say to yourself that you will no longer look for excuses. You will in fact accept the responsibility on a daily basis for your course of action. You will expect positive things to happen and will revel in the rewards. You will also embrace and glean from the negative actions the valuable lessons and apply them to your next endeavor.

If you have anything right now that is driving you towards emotional bankruptcy, it is probably because you have not taken total ownership of it. In addition your struggle is most likely compounded by the fact that you are trying to deal with this alone. Big time need here - - bring God into the picture. He will not only provide you comfort but He will give you vision, insight and the strength to take ownership.

This is when you use the spiritual side of your power source. The spiritual side will calm, strengthen, and support the emotional side. This resource is so infrequently used by most of us, yet it is always available.

When we feel, I can do this on my own and I have made myself what I am today through hard work, we simply have relieved God of that responsibility. If I own something, I have bought and paid for it and it has become an asset. On the other hand, until it is paid for I do not own it and a portion of it is a liability.

Chapter 8

Ownership

The most successful people I know wake up every day knowing what they need, want, and expect. If they don't get them, they create them. Being responsible is a very healthy way to live and requires all three sides of your power source, physical, emotional, and spiritual to achieve.

The premise here is, you cannot keep or get rid of anything you do not own. This not only includes the physical things of our life but the emotional feelings also. There is no greater feeling of ownership than when you have made the last car payment and the car finally belongs to you. Let us take a look at what changes when you finally own it.

>First of all, the net worth is all yours.

>Second, it becomes a great bargaining chip when you want to upgrade.

>Third, it frees up part of your budget to be used elsewhere.

One of the most important ingredients that will assure you of success is your ownership of emotions. The emotional side of your power source is given to many ups and downs. We have all experienced those "power surges" that almost blow out our whole system. It is then that we must reach inside ours hearts and the core of our being and take the ownership of this emotion. Let me give you an example:

My dad was a wonderful source of knowledge and wisdom and I tapped it frequently. He provided me with much support and inspiration that I believed would be there forever. When I was 29 years old, my dad was 57, and I was just beginning to realize the value of his advice and guidance when a heart attack took him from me. Needless to say, I was devastated and hit with an emotional freight train.

I spent too much time in the fear mode of "what am I going to do now?" You see, during that time, I was denying the ownership of that emotion and it crippled me and held me back. I know now if my father could have spoken to me he would have said, "you have all that it takes, own it and be responsible." Don't get me wrong; when something tragic happens in our lives, we need to deal with the negative emotion by embracing it and owning it. What we can't afford to do is to let the emotion own us.

You see, by my action of not owning it, it owned me and I did not have the power to get rid of it. The same three things happen when you own an emotion as does when you finally own that car - It's net worth is ALL yours; It shores up your bargaining power for the next experience ; It frees up your thinking power to invest in the next experience

If you have anything right now that is driving you towards emotional bankruptcy, it is probably because you have not taken total ownership f it. In addition your struggle is most likely compounded by the fact that you are trying to deal with this alone. Big time need here - - bring God into the picture. He will not only provide you comfort but He will give you vision, insight and the strength to take ownership.

This is when you use the spiritual side of your power source. The spiritual side will calm, strengthen, and support the emotional side. This resource is so infrequently used by most of us, yet it is always available.

When we feel, I can do this on my own and I have made myself what I am today through hard work, we simply have relieved God of that responsibility. If I own something, I have bought and paid for it and it has become an asset. On the other hand, until it is paid for I do not own it and a portion of it is a liability.

The sad thing is, we seem to want to pay beyond the end of the contract for our emotions. The good news is that we can stop doing that and become so emotionally healthy that successes we never thought possible will come comparatively easy.

Stop right here and audit your emotional bank to determine its well-being.

Is it healthy? Have you taken ownership of your emotions? Are you turning to your spiritual power source and allowing God to direct your actions?

Important, if this is to be a benefit you must take your time on this.

Chapter 9

Invest

This is a little like the seed in the sack theory - if you do not plant it, it won't grow! The investment I am talking about here goes beyond money or even a required block of time.

When we invest our money, we try and put it where it will earn the most interest. There are several factors that make up our decision such as: How much money do we have to invest? Do I need this money for other things any time soon? Is the investment a high risk? What is the interest rate paid? How long do I have to have it invested before I see some positive return? Can I do this on my own or do I need a broker? If I need a broker, who do I chose? How much commission must I pay the broker?

When we look at the block of time we give to our work as an investment, it carries some of the same requirements as our money investment. How much time are you willing to give? Would this time be better spent somewhere else? What is my risk for investing or not investing? How long do I have to invest my time before I can expect a positive return? Are there others I need to tie into? If I need others, how much are they expecting in return?

As you can see, investing, even in its basic form, requires much thought. Let us now look at investing in an even deeper way. If you expect your life to produce great rewards, then your willingness to invest must come from deep inside your very being and soul. When you approach your life from the point that when you invest yourself for the standard required length of time, you will achieve some level of job security and be able to afford to live at an acceptable standard you have not gone beyond the surface. This of course, is related to attitude. Looking at time and effort is important to put a high sense of desire to the endeavor. When you do this, you will reach deep inside yourself and make a constant and consistent investment.

This level of investment takes the kind of commitment that allows you to say no and realize that at times it is the most positive thing you could do. This comes from a deep burning desire that is fed and supported by our emotional and spiritual power source. Almost always, when an endeavor takes on a lack luster appearance, it is because we did not invest all we had to invest. I realize there are things that require our involvement that do not motivate us to invest all we have to invest. What we must remember is that our level of investment will determine our return. There are literally thousands of stories that exemplify the theory; you should invest 120% of yourself in all endeavors. Let me share a personal experience that supports this.

Several years ago when I was traveling, as a Salesman I had a store I called on that did not use much product and therefore, was on the low end of my client priority list. It was getting late in the day when I came to the town where this client's store was located. I wanted to get to the next town before the client, who was a large account of mine closed his store. I made the decision that the small account probably didn't need anything anyway and drove right on past - saying to myself I would see him next time.

I got several miles down the road when I started thinking about the statements I made to the salespeople I was training. "Never - Never pass up an opportunity to put your product before a client." I started to feel guilty about passing by the small client. I finally made the decision to turn around and go back. When I walked into his store he said, "Wow, am I glad to see you!" It turned out that he had a very large project that he could use one of my products on but didn't know how to bid it. I, of course, helped him work up the bid, which he got, and I got a very large order.

Total investment means you never bail out on the commitment you have made to be there. Important, make sure your motive for making the investment is in line with all phases of your power source.

Going back to how you prepare yourself for the investment. Reach deep inside yourself and become aware of what you have to invest. Spend time meditating and communicating with God so as to see the complete picture. We are all going to make some bad investments - - just remember, in the midst of all the strife and confusion, there is always a new door or window of opportunity. The real loser is the one who simply does not invest what they have been given to invest. The true winner sees their investment as an opportunity to share through an exchange program, their life with others. When this is the motive for your investment, the returns will astound you!

Chapter 10

Focus

This is the action of keeping your plan or vision clear and understandable. In order for this to take place we must actively pursue it (the plan) on a daily basis. Most projects that fail do so because we are not committed to staying focused.

Preparing yourself every day to meet your expectations is very important in staying focused. It is very difficult to stay focused on anything if you have not identified your expectations and have not developed a plan of action. Nothing will deplete your energy more than not having a direction or purpose for your day.

The activity of staying focused requires the use of all of your Power Sources. Aligning your emotional power source with the plan is vital. Only when we are emotionally in tune with the plan, will we stay on board. After all, it is by our emotions that we either enjoy the rewards or suffer the consequences.

When we have a task to perform that we would rather not have to do, it is easy to find, through our emotions, reasons for not doing it. If we are to overcome this dilemma, we must put into play a reward system that motivates us emotionally. It is by emotion that action is instituted.

It is interesting to note that whatever you bring into the game is what you will have to play with. For an example: if you bring in a positive "I want this and I can do this attitude," it will be easy to stay focused on the game.

When you allow your spiritual power source to become involved, it will keep you honest in what you are planning to do. It will also educate your emotional and physical power source on how to do it. Of course, the activity of "How to start your day" will support and prepare you to stay focused on your daily plan.

We have all experienced having a plan that required us to regroup, maybe even start all over again but yet because we stayed focused on the objective we eventually achieved our goal. This took place because you put into play all of the aforementioned activities.

There is an area of caution here. We can't always do what we would prefer to do at a given time. It is important to note that there will be things we need to do for the well being of not only ourselves, but for those around us that we would rather not have to do. The most important part of this type of activity is our commitment to supporting the corporate cause. Zig Ziegler put it best in his book, I will see you at the Top when he said, "You can have anything you want if you will just help enough other people get what they want in the process."

Staying focused is not only being committed to achieving what you want but also supporting and inspiring others to be successful in achieving what they desire. Having a "single minded intensity to achieve" is an attribute when you use it for the benefit of all those involved. However, when you are blind to others needs and ignore their desire to be a part of the process you will reap more consequences than rewards.

When I am presenting "Leadership Workshops" I find the very best leaders are those who spend their time getting and keeping the best people. This is accomplished by surrounding themselves with people that have integrity, knowledge and a basic desire to achieve the objective. In addition, they recognize that people are their greatest commodity and that by their willingness to support and inspire them to go beyond the basic expectations they will feel they have value and have been approved of. Being approved of, either by you or by others, is a very important link to staying focused.

Finally, when we realize that we can have anything we want, not everything we want, we will take the time to prepare by prioritizing those things we need to focus on.

Remember, we need to be a part of developing the agenda and then we will take ownership. When we totally own it, we will stay focused.

Before you go on take some time to *continue* to identify your purpose. Keep in mind the difference between purpose and reason.

My "reason" for doing what I do is to get paid so I can support my family and myself.

My purpose as God has identified for me, is to educate, inspire and encourage people to be the best they can be according to Gods leading and to be willing to share the rewards.

Remember, TAKE YOUR TIME!

Chapter 11

Relationships

The first relationship I want to discuss is the one we have with ourselves. There is a strong word connected to all relationships if we are to do more than survive. That word is COVENANT! What does this mean? In simple terms it means that you will never leave this relationship regardless of the circumstances. We need to take our lead from God in this for He is the same yesterday, today and forever. His arms are never too short and His caring and love is unending. So, when was the last time you saw yourself in a loving, forgiving manner?

Any time we bail out on what we have for gifts/tools we are breaking the covenant we have with ourselves and with God. To say "I believe in me" is vital as long as we realize that this is true because God believes in me. So how about your relationship with others? The same modus operandi applies. Now we must remember that we have many different types of relationships – spousal, children, worker, friend and so forth. The basics of covenant apply in all cases, however the purpose will change.

The real key here is to be able to use your power sources to effectively make a difference in all your relationships. Who you are should make a difference! Question: Is it for the better? Or does it cause others to stumble? This is another case for success testing your actions before taking them. Let me share a personal experience about judging others.

I had just completed a two week session with a company in California settling a labor strike. This was very stressful for it was extremely volatile, so much so that I was required to wear a bulletproof vest. As I was getting on the airplane to fly back to my office I prayed "Father, please seat me beside someone who just wants to sleep as I do." However, when I got to my seat I discovered the person setting next me was an individual who had more tattoos than skin.

Now, I am generally OK with whatever an individual chooses to do with their body but because I was more concerned about ME than anything else I lost sight of the value. My defense was to sit down and get a book to read. I put the book up to my face so close that I did not have to have eye contact with the one setting next to me. I just grabbed the first book in my brief case for the purpose. I obviously was not reading it so I did not discover the title until later. The title of the book was "You Can't afford the Luxury of a Negative Thought." Ironic? I don't think so!

We had barely gotten off the ground when the tattoo man said, "I see you are reading that book too!" I thought, yeah, right. Then he started quoting the book which made me put it down, in amazement, and begin a discussion with him. I soon forgot all of what I had gone through, engaged in a very enlightening conversation, and lost sight of the once distracting tattoos.

As it turns out he was on his way to Dallas to take his final for a Doctorate Degree in Psychology. WOW, what an interesting conversation we had. I learned so much about many different things and he said he did as well. On our approach to the Denver airport I asked him a question that had been on my mind for some time "what is a man of your caliber doing with so many tattoos? His answer which I shall never forget was – "one of the differences between you and I is that some of my past mistakes are still visible." What a profound and strong statement that made me understand where my accountability was.

I soon discovered that whenever we get too centered on ourselves, and we have said to God that we are available, then we need to be prepared for Him to take us seriously. I am truly glad He did.

Judging is dangerous, at best, but when we are caught up in ourselves it is simply disastrous!

Stop reading again and take the time to reflect on this chapter.

Spend some time looking for the positive experiences you have had that started out being negative.

When doing this discover what you did to redirect the flow and also what others did to create the positive atmosphere.

Please remember to take your time.

This book is not meant to be read in a hurry so take time to discover and feel the power sources of your life!!

Positive and Effective Verbal Communication

All of what we have talked about before is absolutely worthless unless we are willing and able to communicate our expectations.

Marriages, corporations, institutions, and personal relationships of all kinds flourish and grow because of quality, open, and positive communications. However it is also true that relationships will wither and dye when faced with the lack of quality, open, and positive communications or from the use of combatant type communications. Nothing, *absolutely nothing*, will impact your success ratio as much as your ability to communicate effectively.

The two basic modes of communication are **verbal** and **non verbal**. We will discuss both in the following chapters starting with the verbal mode.

This is the form of communication we typically use the most yet it is the least productive. The reason for this dilemma is two fold: First, the sender is boring; second, the receiver is unwilling to listen. Have you ever thought of this, "When you speak, what do you want to have happen?" If we could just take the time to figure that out before we ever speak, we would improve our batting average a great deal. I realize this is not always possible for many times we must speak spontaneously and therefore, we lose the listeners.

There are several things that affect how well we are received verbally but none are as important as attitude. Whatever attitude you bring into the conversation, will most likely dictate the outcome. Oh, I know that attitudes can change as the conversation continues but we must realize that the attitude we bring in will be factored into all of the conversation and will have an effect on the outcome.

For an example, if you bring a negative attitude into the conversation and somewhere in the course of it all you change to being more positive, the listener will receive your change in a very guarded way. It will take a longer period of time to accept your change and, in fact, you will find they will have some doubt even at the end of the conversation.

On the other hand, if you bring into the conversation a positive attitude and somewhere in the course of it you become negative, the listener will try and determine what he or she did to cause you to become negative and make every effort to get you back on a positive track. This simply means that you have a maximum of **ten seconds** to either impress or depress your audience.

What I find disconcerting is that we spend a great deal of time working on our ability to communicate in the written form and just allow our verbal form to exist. Here is a ratio that factors into the success of any communication. 90% of the responsibility for the clarity of the message lies in the sender's hands while 10% lies in the receiver's hands. This is supported by the fact that the sender knows what is being said before it is said and the receiver is hearing it for the first time.

The following are ways to exchange negative verbal formats for positive verbal formats:

<u>THINK</u>; Have you taken the time to determine what you want to have happen when you speak. Have you success tested the conversation? The best way to do this is to simply ask yourself this question, "How would I receive this conversation? Would I respond or react?" Remember, responding is always positive and reacting is always negative. Make sure your brain does not go dormant while your tongue continues to spew out verbiage.

This is where your emotional power source and your spiritual power source must direct your physical power source. Be very careful; do not allow your emotional power source to take complete control. It is a fact that our emotions can cause us to have a very caustic and non-productive attitude. If our emotions are negative; we must take the time to be in-tune with our spiritual power source in order to create a more positive demeanor. There is simply no exercise more important than thinking!

<u>PREPARATION</u>; Have you prepared yourself with facts, not just with what others are saying or even worse what YOU think your listener has done or is going to do? I realize our lives are heavily impacted by perceptions. I am more concerned here with the fact that we as the sender have control over the outcome based on how and what we say. A major part of preparation is understanding the temperature and mood of the situation.

There are times when we can say certain things and they will be received well while other times those same statements will totally destroy the conversation. If we prepare ourselves well, we will speak less impetuously and with a greater sense of support. This will ALWAYS produce more positive results.

Make sure and success test your facts. That is, make sure your information is factual before speaking. Remember, it is always more productive to speak in a supportive way rather than in a commanding "you will listen" way. Your tone of voice will play a major role in the success or failure of your conversion. Of course, the attitude you bring into the conversation will impact your tone of voice the most. It is good here to ask the question, "What do I want to have happen?" When you do this you become willing to be flexible.

When you convey a negative atmosphere at the beginning you are generally dealing with one or both of these emotions, anger or mad. You may be wondering what is the difference? There truly is a difference. When you are angry your energy level is at its highest point and if you channel your anger into positive energy flow it will enhance the outcome of the conversation. On the other hand, when you are mad, this represents uncontrollable anger and this is when we say things we did not intend to say and create an atmosphere of "no win!"

In addition this can cause trauma with people who were not involved and who simply happen to be in the way. Remember, anger is a very powerful emotion and it can be used to accelerate a situation to positive heights never thought possible or it can totally destroy any chance of success you have now and for a long time. This is true even when you are responsible for reprimanding someone.

For an example, when you are disciplining a child it is always better to negotiate the change by explaining the value of following the rules. In a system of rewards and consequences, take the time to play up the rewards. If you are leading with an "either or" attitude, you will always get a little less than you expected and just enough to get by. On the other hand when you lead with support and encouragement, you will most often get more than you expected. So you see preparation is vital and you must use a good balance of all three of your power sources.

INTEGRITY & TRUST; there are two types of integrity:

>First, do you have a real sense of belief in what you are about to say? This can be developed through the preparation process.

>Second, what is your integrity with person or persons you are about to speak with?

This, of course, is somewhat determined by how well you know them. If they are complete strangers, we need to imply that we trust them. If in fact, we should not trust them, this will show up real early in the conversion providing we implied to them we did trust at the beginning. If you do not imply trust at the beginning, you will never develop a common bond of integrity. More often than not we go into a conversation with a preconceived feeling of trust or mistrust for the persons we are speaking with. Unfortunately, this is to often determined by what others are saying instead of known facts. I realize we are not always able to get the facts prior to speaking. There is an old adage that applies here "garbage in garbage out - good in good out!" In other words, whatever we put into this conversation, we will most likely get the same out of it. Again, a good balance of all three-power sources is imperative here.

RESPECT; this is a wonderful thing and will probably produce the most results of any of the values. This of course, is an earned commodity. In other words, you cannot buy it or command it. It will come to you only when you give it away first. It is interesting to note that you can respect someone that you do not particularly wish a personal relationship with. Respect is something you must have for yourself first. If you find yourself always complaining, you will also find your self respect and self-esteem to be very low. I once read that you can't love or hate something about someone that you haven't already loved or hated about yourself. This rings true when you consider that we see our children in the eyes of what we know we were. We want to improve on the areas we saw as failures in ourselves and embellish the areas we knew were good about ourselves. This of course, is not earning respect but commanding it. So you see, respect is really allowing people to be who they are.

Respect is also helping others to improve on themselves with positive support, understanding and guidance. There is a tremendous correlation between self-respect and what we discussed in the first chapter about looking inside and the ways to start your day. God intended for us to be happy and prosperous. He has given each of us the tools to achieve this. Our challenge is to accept His direction and to realize that as Lincoln said, " Folks can be about as happy as they chose to be." All of your power sources must be used in good balance here but most importantly we must be in control of our emotional power source.

PRACTICE; Take the time to practice your word skills often. If you are serious about improving your ability to communicate better verbally, then get yourself a tape recorder and practice. I know this may sound silly but it works. Remember, when you're writing, we have word processors that will correct our spelling and grammar. Learn to paint word pictures in the minds of your listeners. Learn to speak graphically and with enthusiasm. Unless you take an active role in improving your speaking ability, you will fall short of the mark every time.

Those of us, who make a living speaking, spend much time practicing what and how we say things. We take into account all of the aforementioned values and constantly strive to improve on them. When you are listening to yourself, be objective and listen for those areas that need improving. Ideally, you should have someone who knows you well, listen and then critique your Presentation. This of course, goes back to the beginning of this chapter and the need to invest yourself in your plan for success. You are in charge so you best act like it!

If you use all five of the aforementioned directives before you engage in verbal conversation, you will enjoy a tremendous amount of positive success. You will also find yourself having to repeat less and you will be less frustrated. Remember, listeners want to listen - - we, as the sender must take the responsibility for the value and clarity of the message. Here is a wonderful filter system that will help keep you out of the ditch and on the hard surface.

The Triple Filter Test

Before you speak about someone try taking the following test.

Filter One: Have you made absolutely sure what you are about to say is the truth?

Filter Two: Is what you are about to say about this person something good?

Filter Three: Is what you are sharing going to be useful to the one you are sharing it with?

If you have answered NO to any of the above questions then you should reconsider saying anything at all. Just remember, "Words once spoken can not be retracted – the damage is done!

> Note: Socrates in ancient Greece first devised this filter system. So you see, It has always been important to be careful what you say to whom.

Here is a very enlightening writing; "Be careful of your thoughts for they become Words! Be careful of your words for they become actions! Be careful of your Actions for they become habits! Be careful of your habits for they form your character! And be very careful of what your character becomes for it will determine your DESTINY! - Anonymous

So, you see words are never just words. Words are very powerful and have the ability to change the face of everything.

Chapter 13

Positive and Effective Non-Verbal Communication

This covers body language, listening, & written skills.

Body Language: This is a form of non-verbal communication that generally supports our real feelings and is the one factor that will determine the success or failure of our endeavor. There are several areas I want to discuss here.

<u>First, Facial Expression:</u> This is the one area we look at the most. We have been told since we were old enough to understand that smiling was a whole lot easier than frowning. Of course, this really depends on the situation and the attitude we bring into it.

Lets take a look at the basic value of the smile. A smile sends a message of happiness and a willingness to support. The smile will create the feeling of integrity and reveal a caring attitude towards the situation. We must remember that in all forms of communication we have no more than four seconds to impress or depress those involved and four seconds is being very generous. In the chapter on verbal communication I talked about what do you want to have happen when you speak. If you are looking for a specific response then you must prepare the prospect to listen and not just hear the noise. Smiling is an invitation to listen.

It is truly important for the smile to be genuine for most people will see through a fake smile and assume that you are up to no good. This gives value to the fact that the genuine smile comes from the emotional power and spiritual power. In other words it must come from your heart. To say you should smile all the time is not realistic or genuine. However, even in those times when smiling isn't a part of the process, when worry has taken over, if you will invest yourself in the situation and keep your mind on the expected outcome; the smile will be there even if it is somewhat anxious.

A smile will prepare you, and the listener, to listen and to take positive action on the message. Those people who say, "I just don't smile very much" need to search their souls to discover what is causing them to feel this way. Nobody is destined to be a grouch; it is a conscious decision on their part. I realize things happen that give us reason to have a negative attitude, which can keep us from smiling, yet I believe it is still our decision as to how we are going to approach the situation. Will you form a smile that empowers you to meet the challenge and find a positive solution or a frown that shackles you and makes you problem bound.

Second, Posture: Standing or sitting, it is very important to control the message we send. Standing or sitting with our shoulders rounded and back bent sends one of two messages, one, we are bored, tired, and disinterested or two, we feel beat and unworthy. I am sure most of you have a time of day when you seem to run out of energy. Mine seems to be around two o'clock in the afternoon. I telegraph my feelings with my posture. I just look tired which also sends a false message of being confused.

I remember a lesson my first speech and voice teacher taught me. If you are singing under the note (flat) or speaking flat, raise your eyebrows. This exercise seems to bring renewed strength and energy to your being. If the situation persists, you may need to stand on your tiptoes. I know it sounds silly but the fact remains it works. My teacher was of the opinion that you had not run out of energy but in fact had become unwilling to continue at the previous pace. I found this to be an interesting concept and after analyzing it, discovered it to be true.

Body language is the precursor to all verbal messages even when the person is not visible. Let us consider the telephone; What ever message your face is portraying your voice will convey. In other words if you are frowning or smiling the person on the other end of the line will know. However, in telephone communications, we must be very aware of how distinct our message is because we are not controlling the elements on the other end of the line.

For an example; how many times have you received a phone call when you were in the middle of something that required your complete attention and yet you attempted to be attentive to both? We need to be willing to share our position with the caller so as to insure a positive result for both. Telephone techniques is another subject altogether and there have been many great books written on the subject. I am not going to go into that part of the process. Let it just suffice to say you should success test your telephone conversations as well and pay attention to the results. You might try putting a mirror in front of your phone - - you will then see what you are about to say!

Body language is sometimes the only way we can communicate. I have a friend who has had a stroke and can't speak or write. Neither he nor I know sign language so if we were to continue our relationship we had to improvise. We have become very good at reading each other's thoughts via body language. It has truly enhanced my ability to communicate both as the sender and the receiver. There is a factor here which needs to be recognized. If he and I weren't dedicated to continuing our relationship, we would not have made the effort to continue our communications . I wonder how many opportunities we miss to grow spiritually, emotionally, and physically because we just don't have the dedication to allocate the extra time it takes?

When I am speaking with a group, large or small, I immediately pick out several people in the audience whom I can key on. My criteria for choosing these key people are always determined by body language first. If they are sitting up straight and are concentrating on what is about to happen I key on them first. As I get into my presentation I determine those who are really excited about "listening" and "participating" and then I key on them. The purpose for this is to give me a sense of positive feed back and keeps the fire burning in me to produce. This same feeling and exercise should be instilled whenever we speak. Just remember to speak enthusiastically and listen calmly.

This part of communication is so important for you. Where as it is important what you say, it is infinitely more important what your body language is saying. What ever your body portrays, your tongue will profess, whatever body language you bring into the conversation, will dictate the probable success or failure of the conversation.

Often if you are upset and initiate the conversation with a stern face supported by a tense and rigid body, you will cause the listener to immediately put up their defenses. This will also cause them to listen just long enough to determine what you want and probably decide that your request is not valid or at least unfair. Therefore, if you are trying to get something accomplished, you have already diminished the chances for success by 80%. I realize there are times when this kind of body language is appropriate. This is when you are not looking for any specific results from positive action you are just letting them know that you are irritated and you want them to feel your wrath. Be careful of this kind of action because they will remember it the longest. That is, they will factor that attitude in the next time you get conversationally involved and this will most likely become a major barrier to your future interactions.

The best example I can give happened some time back when I was doing some major consulting for a large firm. Part of what I was doing was helping the upper management discover where the glitches were. There was a major communication stale mate between one of the largest divisions and the upper management. I discovered after talking with several of the employees of that division, that several months prior, things had gone sour in their division. The individual who was in charge of that division apparently got so frustrated that he came unglued and vented his uncontrollable anger on the staff. Now every time he walks into the department and tries to convey a message, they remember his anger and therefore, only hear about 10% of what he has to say. They watch his body language to see if it in any way resembles what it was like when he vented. He has already demonstrated to them that he is capable of doing this so they almost expect him to do it again. This kind of situation can happen and you don't even realize it. Lets look at what can be done to avoid this and also what can be done after the fact to rectify it.

Avoid it: In this particular situation, the division head could have called some key people into his office to discover what they felt was taking place. Sometimes things get headed in the wrong direction and nobody knows how to stop them. When you pick out key figures and share with them your concern, you not only create a larger think tank but also give those you have chosen a feeling of importance. This will generally create within them a strong desire to resolve. In essence, I am saying, turn over a few more rocks before you start firing your canon. After all, once you have fired you are left with no bullets and a smoking gun.

Fix It: What to do if you have lost control and fired your canon. This is a difficult situation but the operative words here are "humility, accountability, and ownership," An unsolicited apology will do wonders in mending fences. The most important part of the apology must be that it is genuine. Do not start off giving them a reason why you exploded in the first place. You must be willing to accept the full responsibility for your actions. It really makes no difference if you felt you were just in your actions or not. The recipients want to simply know that you made an error and that you are sorry for your hasty action.

When you are able to humble yourself to that degree you will mend the fence and restore the confidence between your people and yourself. Again, remember what your objective was in the first place. The main objective here is to not let righteous indignation destroy the integrity bond you have with your people. This of course, applies when it is your personal relationships as well as with your work relationships.

When we look at the human aspect of this, we will realize that at some time we will allow our anger to turn to being frustrated and mad and we will vent in a seemingly uncontrollable way. The real pain here is not the fact that we have allowed ourselves to fall into this trap but it is if we don't recognize the need to assess the damage and rectify it by taking full responsibility. This demands a very delicate balance of all our power sources. Those people who seem to always win are those who spend a great deal of time honing their skills in the use of their power sources. They also realize this is a constant thing and that they must adjust the temperature and attitude regularly. Of course all of this takes practice - practice - practice!

Listening: If there is any one area that we could all improve on, that would increase our productivity, it would be listening. This is the area we should spend the most time on yet we often spend the least amount of time on it.

This dilemma is caused primarily by the fact that we like to talk and we like to control the conversations. Besides, listening is boring and it means we must concentrate. It is compounded further by the fact that I must clear my mind, become calm and quiet, be open, and prepare myself to receive. When you look at this, it doesn't seem like it should be so difficult. It is difficult because, by nature, we are control freaks. What is really sad is that we don't realize that when we become good listeners we are more in control than when we are talking. You see knowledge begets strength - strength begets control - you gain knowledge by listening not by talking.

When I am directing a sales workshop, I share with the participants that if they must speak then ask a question. Then of course, exercise the ability to listen to the answer. An interesting fact is that knowledge does not make you wise. Wisdom comes in knowing what to do with the knowledge. When we listen intently and gain the knowledge, we can speak with wisdom and create positive action.

One of the major dilemmas in listening is the art of selective listening. That is listening only to the parts that we thoroughly understand and make us feel good. This also means taking it to the level of listening only to those whom we like and even then listening only when we are in the mood to do so. Another factor in this is belief. That is, how much faith we have in the speaker. Do we believe he or she has the expertise to speak about the subject matter? If they are a complete stranger, we struggle with the belief part. This can be softened if someone you trust is there to recommend his or her integrity.

One of the main roadblocks to our willingness to listen is when we feel we know as much about the subject as the speaker and ever more destructive is when we feel we know more than the speaker. Sometimes we feel that a person must have a certain status in order for us to believe them. A prime example of this happened to me several years ago when I was speaking at a high school teacher in-service. I always ask the person introducing me to make it brief, most people really do not want to hear about all the great things the speaker has done. On this occasion the person introducing me did keep it brief, however, I was astounded as she began to close and asked the audience to help her welcome Dr. Said. WOW, that was the fastest Doctorate degree in history.

Here's what happened. It immediately set a negative defensive mood for me. I knew there had to be someone in the audience who knew me and knew I did not have a doctorate degree. I also felt that they were now expecting more than I could deliver. Now, how could I salvage this situation and not embarrass the person who introduced me even though I wanted to do so. I decided to make my presentation with as much energy and enthusiasm as always and let the chips fall as they may. I knew if I went out there and tried to explain the situation it would take the whole time I was allotted and then I am not sure it would have been resolved.

The presentation was very well received in fact I received a standing ovation. Afterwards I went to the person who introduced me and asked why she had done that? She replied that she knew her staff and they would not have believed what I had to say unless I had doctorate credentials. I just couldn't believe that basis of thinking. It is interesting to note that I asked one of the other coordinators to share with me any feedback they received from the participants. This person informed me some time later that the consensus of opinion was that the message was the best message they had ever heard at an in-service but found it hard to believe that anyone with a doctorate degree in education could be that dynamic. Once again proving that truth is so much greater than fiction.

Why do we listen?

A. We seek knowledge about a certain subject. In this situation we have a specific agenda. We are looking for specific information and are willing to search out the people who will provide if for us.

B. We are in a two-way dialog with someone we trust. In this situation it makes no difference if the dialog is friendly or argumentative; we will listen because of trust and without regard to probable consequences.

C. Someone higher on the pecking order than us tells us to. This often has a very low retention level. Most of us do not want to be told to listen. As children when our parents asked us if we were listening to them, we always said yes even when we really weren't. Unfortunately, as adults we do the same thing.

D. We have a high level of interest in the person or subject about whom they are speaking and our curiosity makes us listen. This will generally have great positive results. However, be aware that this is the arena in which gossip is born.

It is good to keep in mind this great quote, "Great People talk about ideas! Average People talk about things! Small People talk about other people!" Gossip is defined this way. If it is being told to you and it is not about you and you were not there and you decide to repeat it then it is gossip. Remember, the triple filter system.

We must remember that just because we hear the speaker speaking does not mean we listen to what they are saying. You see, in the normal course of a day, we are subjected to a huge amount of words, noise, and actions. We also have this unique filtering system that allows us to determine what part of what we are listening to is valuable to us.

Caution: If your original agenda is narrow in its scope you will most likely miss a great opportunity to grow in knowledge.

Let me give you an example of what I am talking about. This I am sure is a familiar scene to all of us. You have come into a room where the conversion has already started. The person talking is speaking about a subject you know nothing about and even worse you have never thought you wanted to know about it. It appears that everyone else is hanging on the speakers every word. What is the first thought that goes through your mind? Most likely "how did I get in here and where is the exit?"

There are several reasons why we feel that way. First, we are embarrassed about our lack of knowledge of the subject. We have this feeling that everybody in the room will think we are dumb. Second, we feel the subject is boring. Third, we know of the subject but it truly is of no interest to us. Lets look at the catalyst of each of these reasons.

While we may feel embarrassed about our lack of knowledge on the subject the main motive is our inability to participate. Most of us feel the need to contribute to the conversation. The fear of appearing "dumb" is very real. Nobody wants to be seen that way. The real unfortunate part of this is that the feeling is generally self-generated. We would probably be amazed at how many people who are in the situation feel the same as we do.

Often when we feel a subject is boring, it is because we don't understand and it is out of our needs realm. It is good to remember that more times than not the subject is not boring but maybe the speaker is.

Knowing of the subject but genuinely having no interest is the positive part of our filtering system. We must take the responsibility to realize what areas we will invest ourselves in and make a positive contribution.

You can apply this same analogy to one on one conversation. Have you ever wondered why some people seem to be able to glean things from any conversation? It is most likely because they operate on the premise that even if they don't understand the subject they can at least form a series of questions that will help them understand. You can hear without participating but you cannot listen without participating.

I believe that listening is the most important phase of our communication skills. I further realize it is the area in which we spend the least amount of time perfecting. I suppose there are several reasons why this is true. However, I feel that not knowing how to improve far out distances all the rest. Let me share with you a process including specific exercises that will greatly enhance your listening ability.

Caution: This will seem simple in its context but believe me you will find it quite difficult to implement.

This first step in acquiring a new found ability to listen is to develop a keen sense of desire to do so. Most of us are getting along okay the way we are so why wander into an area we don't understand and feel we can't change. When you consider the catalyst for creating this desire comes from our emotional and spiritual power source, we can understand why it is so difficult. I realize that the strongest reason for not increasing my desire to listen is that my plate is already full and if I listen I must take action.

Lets begin this process by doing the following exercise:

First; take the time right now to list all the subjects you feel comfortable conversing about and find interesting and necessary to your well being.

Second; list the subjects that you are frequently exposed to that you don't deem interesting or necessary to your well being.

Third; list the subjects that you would like to be more knowledgeable about knowing they would support your personal agenda. Please put the book down and do this exercise right now. Take plenty of time to do this.

Now that you have completed this part of the exercise look at the first list and answer the following questions objectively:

How broad is my scope?

How much do I really know about these subjects?

Do I know someone who I am in frequent conversion with that if I would listen more intently, I would hear and grow in knowledge of these subjects?

Am I not listening to this person because of personal reasons: (stature, race, position, gender and etc)?

Does my present scope of listening provide for me the substance to achieve my life goals?

Please don't just answer these questions verbally to yourself but write them down on a separate sheet of paper. Be very truthful with your answers for only you will either win or lose in this exercise. Take the time to really reflect on your answers. Give yourself the credit where you are doing well and challenge yourself to improve in areas you are weak.

Take a look at the second list and put a star beside the ones that you think might have a positive impact on your life achievement process.

Next prioritize the stared ones starting with number one as to which ones you are going to include in your program of life achievements.

Look at the third list and again prioritize them with a number system starting with one as to their level of importance.

On another sheet of paper, copy down the stared ones from list number two in order of importance and add them to list number three.

From this list chose one to three subjects you are going to invest yourself in now.

You have identified desire and you will find time in your present time agenda to make them work. Doing this exercise is only the first step in the process. What you have done here is to prepare yourself with a plan. In other words, you have created a desire to achieve.

Unfortunately, many plans that are put down on paper never get any farther. In order for this to be more than a good looking plan, you must do the hard part and take action NOW!

The next step is to find people who are knowledgeable of the final selected subjects, put yourself in position to glean their knowledge by listening to them either in person or by extended communication, (letters, books, phone, e-mail, Internet, audio-video tapes Cd's). It is imperative that you make a spot for this activity in your present time agenda, be faithful to it, and be consistent. In order for this to take place, we must concentrate on the objective by keeping the BIG picture in front of us and the daily steps within us every day.

You see this is no different than the action required to close a sale. There must be a benefit for me. Identify the benefits of listening more intently - do the work - revel in the rewards. It is important to note, that in order for your physical power source to support this issue you must tap into your emotional and spiritual power sources for without a clear cut go signal from them you will not take the action.

It is my ardent hope and prayer that having done this exercise you have experienced many revelations. I further hope and pray that you are now embarking on a journey of listening with new and renewed strength and vision.

Be it known that the road will be rocky at best. Be very aware of the potholes and bumps. Remember, they are merely speed bumps and they can only slow you down not stop you completely - for only you can do that.

Written Communications: With the discovery of e-mail and fax machines, this mode of communication has changed considerably. I am not going to spend a lot of time on this aspect of communications but will address some of the important areas

1.) Structure or make up: It is very important that your communique is in the right form. If a formal letter is called for, then it should be structured as such. If it is in the form of a memo, then that structure and make up should be used. Generally, when it is a memo, it is shorter in its content.

2.) What should be taken into consideration before developing the text:
    A. Who are you and what is your role in this endeavor?
    B. Who are you sending it to and what is their role in this endeavor?
    C. What are you expecting to have happen from the communication?
    D. What is the receiver's ability to comprehend?
    E. Is there a response needed and if so what is the time line?

3.) Text content:
- A. Make sure it is information, which is data crunched down into usable form.
- B. Make it concise and to the point.
- C. Use understandable words. If the receiver has to refer to Webster to understand, they probably will not.

Remember, the written word as well as the spoken word is subject to this dilemma - - "I know you think you understand what I said - - What you don't realize is that what I said is not what I meant!"

Billboards and signs are a very powerful example of how the written word can stimulate thought and action. Here are just a few examples.

> Seen on the outside reader board of a church in south Texas in the middle of July. "You think it is HOT here!"

> A sign on a convents high security fence. "Absolutely no trespassing - violators will be prosecuted to the letter of the law - - Sisters of Mercy

> Sign on the side of dairy "Our milk does not come from contented cows - - Our cows are striving to do better every day!"

> Seen on a tee shirt as well as a church bill board - - "There are no parties in Hell - - only one big bar-be-que and you do not want to be invited!"

The introduction of e-mail has made our communications more conversational and that is probably a positive. I just caution you that the same rules apply here as they do in the regular written and spoken form.

All aspects of communication are very important. It is imperative that we pay attention to the results we are getting from each aspect and then use these results to practice, study and grow. Develop a good balance of your "Power Sources" and you will be astounded at the results.

There simply is no replacement for personal inner-action. As I have said above, all forms of communication are important. However, when we meet face to face the level of understanding and the probable success ratio goes up dramatically.

The great communicators of this world know they can move mountains, change the course of most everything, and achieve the impossible. They know that their talent and expertise is a free gift from God. They also realize that they must be constantly aware of how they are communicating and spend an inordinate amount of time honing their skills.

We have a choice to be either a thermometer or a thermostat. As a thermometer we can only tell what the temperature is. However, as a thermostat we have the power to change it, the scary part is that we can change the climate up or down.

The following test will help you determine just how well you have been communicating:

Think back to the last six conversations you have had where you had a specific objective in mind.

Now success test these conversations with the following formula:

Take plenty of time to do this and record your answers on paper.

1. Who was I speaking with?

2. What was my objective?

3. What was the climate at the time? Open - Closed?

4. What was my attitude going into the conversation?

5. What if any was the excess baggage I brought into this conversation from the last one?

6. Was there a sense of urgency in my voice?

7. Based upon what my objective was, how successful was the endeavor?

8. Based on my answer to number 7, what can I expect the next time I enter into a conversation with this same person or persons?

9. What are the specifics I need to change in order to insure a more successful endeavor the next time?

10. What are the actions I need to do more of in order to enhance the success ratio of my conversations?

Now that you have success tested one of your last conversations, I suggest that you do this periodically. This will definitely help you become a more effective communicator.

Chapter 14

Using Your Time Wisely

All of what we have discussed in the previous chapters has been in preparation for this. It is now time to allocate the resources you have gained in order to prepare a plan of action and put it into motion.

I know we have all heard some old sayings such as " You have all the time there is" and "You can't invest your time in a bank and get more tomorrow." These are all true, however, I want to take it a step further. Our obsession with time, especially the fact that we do not have enough, is the real core of our dilemma. Time management is a matter of planning, staying focused, being flexible, and being disciplined as to how we use it.

1. Planning: Are you a list maker? Do you prioritize your lists? Do you make them daily? Do you use yesterdays list in making today's list? Do you check off the projects as you accomplish them?

2. Staying focused: Do you do the most important things first? Do you stay on board until the project is complete? Do you remind yourself of the reward for completion often? Do you take an occasional five-minute vacation in order to freshen your focus?

3. Be flexible: Do you schedule your time so tight that any change will upset the whole day? Are you willing to exchange one project for another when called to do so?

4. Being disciplined in the process: Do you concentrate on the first three steps? Do you success test your plans (lists) daily? Do you take the time to reward yourself everyday for your successes?

Planning takes some of the guesswork out of our day. It is acceptable some days to have nothing to do and no place to go for this is the time to regroup. However, if you have much to do and feel like you are getting nothing done and going nowhere, you need to revisit your original plan. Nothing will deaden your power sources more then having much to do and feeling like you can't get it done.

On the other hand, I do not do "nothing" very well. I have a friend who recently retired and he made this statement to me. I have nothing to do and it is noon and I have it half done. At first I found this humorous but soon heard the real message. That is, "I feel worthless!" Planning is vital.

Staying focused is sometimes difficult because our interest level wanes. When you do your most important things first, it sometimes leaves only those tasks that we would rather not do. This is when you must instill your creativity and make those tasks interesting. If you don't, you will invariably bring them into the next day and if you do that long enough you won't have any time to do those important tasks.

Being flexible will give you the most reserve of energy possible. When we schedule ourselves so tight that nothing can get in our way, we are doomed to crumble. It also provides us with the best opportunities, which we would have missed if we weren't flexible. Being flexible will help you live longer!

Being disciplined to complete your tasks is vital. We have all kinds of discipline put upon us daily by society in general. However, the one discipline that can really make a difference is the discipline we are willing to self-administer. There are so many things that get in the way of being well disciplined with our time.

The following are just a few:

1. Daydreaming.
2. Low self esteem
3. Not being approved of
4. Not interested in the project
5. Putting our needs before others
6. Needing to get the credit
7. Feeling not needed
8. Being overwhelmed with the process
9. Not understanding its level of importance

I read somewhere that time means, "To Implement My Energies" and I couldn't agree more. The greatest time management tool is to have a plan, be flexible and follow the plan.

There is a story I love to tell when teaching "Time Management" to salespeople. It seems there was a salesman who was always late for his appointments and it was starting to get in the way of his success. His sales manager was getting a little tired of making excuses for him with the clients. He, the sales manager, told the salesman that if he messed up the next appointment because he was late then he should just keep on going for his job would be no longer there.

The salespersons next appointment was the following day in a neighboring town. He knew just how long it took to get there and to the clients office so he gave himself just a couple of minutes to spare. When he arrived at the clients office he could find no place to park except a no parking zone. He drove around the block several times and finally in desperation he parked in the no parking zone. He wrote a note and put it on the windshield of his car. The note said this "Dear officer; I have driven around this block twenty times and I was unable to find a parking space other than this one. If I did not park here I would be late for my appointment and probably lose the sale and my job, Forgive us our trespasses!"

When he returned to his car after the appointment he found a citation attached to his windshield with a note that said, "I have walked around this block for twenty years and if I don't issue this citation I will definitely lose my job, Lead Us Not Into Temptation!"

The real message to this story is "lack of planning on your part does not constitute an emergency on my part!"

Chapter 15

Developing a Plan of Action

Before we learn the process we need to understand that we all have certain HOT BUTTONS!

These are located at the core of our "Power Source" namely in our heart. We all have four basic HOT BUTTONS that affect our lives daily. The following are those four buttons.

1. <u>Recognition</u>, specifically name recognition. This is to say; we want people to recognize us and call us by name. This instills a great sense of belonging and a feeling of being needed.

2. <u>Approval</u>, all of us want to be approved of. Some people wait their whole lives and never get approval.

3. <u>Positive reinforcement</u>, this is the action we crave for others to give to us. This will make us go to the starting line with winning in mind.

4. <u>Identified rewards</u>, this supports the value that we all listen to the same radio station every morning it's call letters are WIFM, "what's in it for me." I am willing to invest myself providing there is a probable reward for my action.

When I am teaching a leadership class, I share with the participants that knowing your people and recognizing them every day is a very powerful tool in getting more done than you expected. It is also interesting to discover how many people are contrary to the plan just because they have never received approval even from their parents, friends and fellow workers.

This is a condition only the person experiencing it can get over. It requires first of all a willingness to admit they are dealing with it. Once they have done that, they can get on with receiving it and accepting it. You see many times it isn't that they aren't getting the approval, it is that they are so used to wanting it they don't recognize it when they get it. If we wallow in our self need long enough, it becomes a veritable jail, shackles and all. Some of us need more positive reinforcement than others. The fact remains however, that we all need it to some degree.

When you hear others say that your presence is very important and that you contribute a great deal to the process, it will empower you to reach even higher. Of course we all want to be rewarded for our efforts. I share with most groups that I simply love to do what I do but I will not do it for nothing. The most lasting rewards are not necessarily the monetary ones. Often times, that pat on the back or that statement in your pay envelope that says you were extra special at a specific time will really empower you to stretch yourself beyond just performing. These are the things that help us stay focused on all of our power sources and stay steadfast to WHO we are. With that in mind lets learn how to develop a quality plan and then become accountable in bringing it to fruition.

Before we get into the mechanics of making a plan and setting goals I want to talk about Vision. You see vision must come before the plan or the plan has no purpose. The following will help you understand what I am talking about.

VISION

V - - - - Visualize
    A. Make a mock up of your objective.
    B. Place it where you must see it daily.

I - - - - Internalize
    A. Speak it out often.
    B. Make acting on it a habit.

S - - - - Strength
    A. See this as your source of empowerment
    B. Lean on it to keep your eyes focused upward.

I - - - - Initiate
    A. Do more than talk - CREATE!
    B. Success test what you have created.

O - - - - Opportunity
    A. Fix this in your mind
    B. Each day is a new window of time to invest in.

N - - - - Never
    A. Allow others to put road- blocks in your way.
    B. Lose sight of God's involvement.

"Where there is no vision the people parish!"
                      Proverbs 29:18

When you are determining your Vision, try and see it in these increments: Six months, one year, and five years.

Making a plan is discovering this, "Where am I going?" Who am I going to meet?" and "What am I going to do when I get there?" Before you can complete this there are some things you must do to prepare yourself for the plan.

1.) Make a list of all the people you feel are successful.

2.) Now from that list set aside those who you know personally.

3) Determine why you feel they are successful.

4.) Define success as you see it for you.

5.) Set aside some time to go visit with the ones you know personally. Pay particular attention to how they handle themselves and what they deem important.

6.) Determine what attributes they have that you would like to have some of. Keep in mind that you are you and they are who they are. Your objective is to fine tune you not become somebody else!

Once you have done the above six steps, take plenty of time to allow the value of the exercise to take root.

Question: When you were listing the people whom you felt were successful did you list yourself? If you do not believe in you and know yourself to be successful then all the rest will just be words with no action.

Now move to the next step in your plan. Take your time.

1.) Make a list of all your abilities. Be good to yourself!

2.) Make a list of all your limitations. Be as honest as possible here.

3.) From your list of limitations, cross-reference your abilities so as to diminish your limitations and discover that they are sometimes your strength.

4.) From the limitations that are left, decide if you want to acquire the expertise to overcome them if so determine what it will take to do so and set the plan in motion. Those that are left from that list let them go, in other words, highlight them and push the delete button.

You are now ready to start determining what you want to do.

1.) Make a list of all the things that come into your mind not being concerned if they are possible or not.

2.) From this list chose several It is best to chose some that you feel are possible for you to do and also some that seem impossible.

3.) List each of those you have chosen in step two separately giving plenty of space to write your action plan.

4.) Take each chosen objective and develop a plan of action that has steps you can take immediately. Nothing will derail your plan quicker then saying, "Someday I'll do it."

Now that you have done this, make sure that all of your objectives are tied to your Vision. You probably have some goals that are possible to achieve immediately and I am sure you have some that will take longer, maybe even forever.

When looking at your short-range goals, make sure they tie to some long-range goal. Short-range goals should be stepping-stones to long range objectives. You will find it beneficial if you arrange them in a progressive flow chart. This should be something you can reference daily. Just remember the goals are steps you are taking to make your vision a reality.

Accountability and You

Now it is time to make ourselves accountable to the plan we have created. This step is the most vital step of all.

1.) Find someone whom you have a great relationship with and respect his or her judgment. Make sure they have also gone through the exercise. Remember the purpose of this is to keep each other accountable to achieving.

2.) Set aside some time to meet with this person for the express purpose of sharing with each other your vision, goals and the plan to achieve.

3.) Once you have shared with each other make a copy of your vision and goals then exchange them with your sharing partner.

4.) Make a commitment to communicate with this sharing partner once a week, for the first month, once every other week during the second month, and then once a month from then on. The express purpose of this step is to ask each other "How are you coming with your steps/goals? Has your vision changed?"

I promise, if you will remain dedicated to this, you will achieve more than you ever thought possible.

This of course requires a continued desire and discipline to improve your current situation. When you feel discouraged the question to ask yourself is, "What you were doing before – how was that working for you? Do I really want more out of life? Am I ready to invest all of my power sources to achieve the maximum of what God has for me? Do I believe in Jeremiah 29-11: *"For I know the plans I have for you, declares the Lord, plans to prosper you and not to harm you, plans to give you Hope and a future."*

SUCCESS FORMULA

-The formula for a successful life is as follows-

IDENTIFIED VISION/GOALS

MAINTAINED DIRECTION

DETERMINED EFFORT

NECESSARY SACRIFICE

PASSION

COURAGE

ACTION

I have just taken you through the process of Identifying your Vision and setting your Goals. If you follow that procedure you will have a plan.

<u>Maintained Direction</u> will be supported by your commitment to the process. The fuel for this action will be found in the core of your Power Source coupled with your willingness to invest it. That willingness will be governed by how genuine you are about achieving the objective in the first place. We all can get caught up in what society thinks we should do and who they think we should be. This is why it is so important to have begun this journey to discover just what you are made of. One thing is for certain, you should never compromise your values for the sake of anything.

Determined Effort is simply that you just won't quit. When you feel you have done everything you can, just remember you haven't. Sometimes it is necessary to take two steps back and reassess the situation. Then move forward with renewed vigor. When I said to my dad that I had tried everything I could he would always answer, "No you haven't." Even though I did not like this I soon realized he was right.

Necessary Sacrifice, in all things there is a cost. Sacrifice is not always painful and in fact when coupled with passion it is almost always joyful! This equates to the investing process I talked about in an earlier chapter. This is also the beginning of taking the process to the level of actually happening. I know this is an unfriendly word to most people but just try and think of it as the stuff that makes happen what you want to have happen. Stress can be a major source of energy or a tremendous drain of energy.

Lets take a look at the two ways of dealing with stress. The stress I am talking about is the kind that has caused your plate to overflow.

    The most common way to deal with stress.

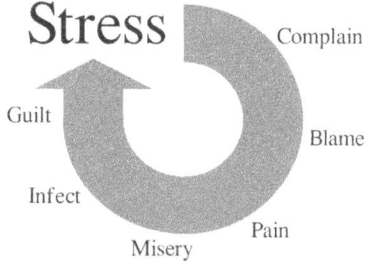

This will always make you feel like you are on a treadmill and going nowhere. This is the main cause of frustration and can very frankly kill you. My cardiologist tells me that the cemetery is full of "It is Just Stress!"

A better way of dealing with stress.

This will provide you with the fuel you need to achieve anything you set out to do. Just remember, that you can do all things when you seek Gods face first and follow his directions.

Dealing with stress in a better way will also give you that great sense of being free and allow you the most precious time you need to become all God intended you to be. Just remember that when you are willing to sacrifice, you are putting yourself in the best position to receive the greatest rewards.

Now, aside from to the two methods for dealing with stress there are two ways to rid your life of stress. First, die! This is something we will all do someday, but I simply do not want to accelerate the action. Second, stick your head in the sand. Question, What is the only thing left sticking up when your head is in the sand? Pretty obvious isn't it? Most people will see this as an easy target and won't resist giving it a boot! Truthfully stress is an important factor to our energy source and is vital to our success.

Passion, nothing is achieved at the optimum level unless passion is a part of it. This is the burning desire deep in your soul that provides you with the power to excel. This passion is acquired by tapping into your "Spiritual Power Source". Striking the match everyday and setting your passion on fire is your responsibility. However, when you let go and let God direct you, you will find an unquenchable fire that will lift you to levels you never new existed. The most exciting part of letting God direct your passion is that He has already success tested it and it comes with a guarantee to work making it a joy to pursue. Passion empowers you to wake up in the morning ready to meet the day with renewed strength, energy and a belief in what you are about to do. After all when you have a passion for life and what you do others will see this and your passion will become contagious.

ATTITUDE IS CONTAGIOUS! MAKE SURE YOURS IS WORTH CATCHING!

Courage, this is an ingredient that is more vital to your success than most people realize. Courage is that inner feeling that makes you steadfast to what you believe. It also provides the right stuff when you must risk it all. When you put it all on the line it takes courage to create that investment. When we get side lined in our process of achieving, more often than not, you can attribute it to our lack of courage to continue in the face of defeat. It also takes courage to not quit on the brink of a miracle. When you step off the ledge of your present comfort zone with courage, God will provide a soft landing place and empower you to continue moving forward. When we give up and say it can't be done those doing it generally interrupt us.

Action, is generally self-explanatory. Once you have done the other steps, it is time to go to the starting line and begin the journey. It never ceases to amaze me the number of people I meet that can do all the right planning, have all the right tools, but are afraid to take the action. This is where I believe that courage comes in. It takes a good measure of courage to step out and risk what you own. It is easy to risk what someone else owns. Courage comes from that inner fire created by passion.

Courage is also a product of your emotional and spiritual power source. If you are having trouble getting started, take the time to look deep into yourself and commune with God for the vision and courage. This is not something you can paint on in the morning. It must come from inside your very being and soul. All the great achievers regardless of their endeavor possess a great understanding of their inner self and are able to stay firm within themselves. Almost all will tell you that it comes from a deep understanding of their "Spiritual Power Source!"

People ask my wife "Where does Cliff get all this information?" Her stock answer is that he lives his life and pays attention. This is all part of becoming aware and in tune with the total you, especially the inner you and your spiritual and emotional power. We are all called to do different things and we are all given gifts to accomplish them. The real secret lies in searching for the gifts, finding them, unwrapping them, sharing them for the good of all people, and ultimately for the glory of God! A good Christian friend of mine put it this way, "If we pay attention to what God has in store for us while here on earth, when our time comes to meet our maker face to face we won't have to ooze under the door with our clothes smelling like smoke!"

Remember, motivation is a personal thing and inspiration is a shared thing. We all need to take on the responsibility to motivate ourselves and also to inspire others to be the best they can be. Caution, make sure you inspire them to be the best they choose to be not to become what and who you want them to be. This, of course, is all about attitude. The thing to remember about attitude is that whatever attitude you wake up with and decide to have today, good or rotten, they both work! "Attitude is Contagious - Make sure yours is worth catching!"

God has put us on the earth for specific purposes. Primarily to serve Him and our fellow man. When we tap into all of our "Power Sources" and allow God to lead us, we will realize success beyond measure.

Life is not easy; it is not without pitfalls, pain and sorrow. It is, however, full of joy, happiness, and incredible love. We are called to embrace it all and to not let life itself become a terminal disease. In order to safeguard against this, I suggest you start your day by thanking God for the opportunities that are coming and end your day by thanking Him for the opportunities experienced. This is a good way to begin journaling.

As you have taken time to read this book and do the exercises it is my hope and prayer that you have been inspired to move forward regardless of your circumstances. Age is not a barrier only your attitude. Attitude will either rocket you into the realms of unimaginable success or imprison you in a quagmire of despair.

"Attitude not Aptitude will determine your Altitude!"

Excuses do not count; only results. When you are climbing your ladder of success it is very important to determine if it is against the right building. When you get to the top it is too late so take the time to success test your life.

If you seek God's face first and know that He wants the very best for you as you want for your children then you will be assured the success you desire.

1. <u>A Cling On!</u>
a) Not willing to let go of present experiences. Feels change and exchange impossible.
b) Causes one to spend their time rearranging the deck chairs on the Titanic
c) Displays bitterness and becomes stagnant.
d) Keeps one from even being considered for the starting line

2. <u>A Spectator!</u>
a) Wants to watch others doing things and criticize.
b) Wants the rewards without being involved with the action.
c) Their In-action is motivated by fear of failure.
d) Does not want to be a part of the starting line up.

3. <u>A Participant!</u>
a) Willing to get involved on a limited basis. (only what is required)
b) Wants to be seen as one who is willing.
c) Does not want to be singled out and is reluctant to be a leader.
d) Is willing to accept their role and collect their portion.

4. <u>A Contributor!</u>
a) Has some good ideas and is willing to share.
b) Has a need to be recognized.
c) Is a definite asset to the team.
d) Wants to be a leader, struggles with how but is willing to learn.

5. <u>An Investor!</u>
a) Is willing to risk for the sake of the team.
b) Is always willing to do the "and then some."
c) Demonstrates top quality Leadership/Coaching skills.
d) Has little need for personal recognition!
e) Is always focused on the bottom line to support the company!

Note: All of us will occasionally spend time in each of the above. The secret to celebrating success is to spend 95% of your time as an investor. This will provide many Wow experiences!

Takers: Takers are a combination of Participant and Contributor. Their focus is themselves and their motive is selfish and self-centered. They listen to the radio station WIFM - (What's in it for me.) before taking action.

Givers: Givers are a combination of Contributor and Investor. Their main issue is to encourage and inspire the team around them. They need no recognition for their word and work are stamped with TRUTH & EXCELLENCE!

It is my feeling that we should spend approximately 95% of our time as a contributor /investor, balance is what we are looking for here. When you realize that learning never stops then you can see the correlation between the learning and investing.

Life is about lessons. Once you have learned the lesson you will get another one. I do not intend to arrive at deaths door with any energy left over. I intend to arrive totally spent and saying, "WOW! WHAT A TRIP!"

It is very necessary for you to have a brief detailed statement as to how you are going to live your life. In other words a "Personal Mission Statement." By having this and coupling it with your identified purpose statement you will be able to find that much eluded balance with your "Power Source!"

The following is my Mission Statement. Make sure you use this as a guide line only - your statement needs to speak to your needs which will inspire you to achieve great things.

CLIFF SAID'S PERSONAL MISSION STATEMENT

Proverbs 29:18 "Where there is no vision the People Perish!"

I will always put God and my family first.

I will seek a balance between my work and my family.

I will strive every day to learn something new and seek ways to apply this new knowledge.

I will be a contributor to life and to those around me daily.

I will accept the role of "teacher" as God has called me to do so.

I will begin each day with a time set aside to communicate with God about His plans for me.

I will be a self-starter every day with a purpose in mind and the willingness to expend the effort to achieve it.

I will strive to be a better listener each day and I will concentrate on hearing what I am listening to.

I will look for the humor in all my experiences and I will laugh each day.

I will involve myself in some charitable task each day and I will not be found out. If I am found out it doesn't count.

Moreover, I will invest my time, talent and resources so as to create a positive experience for all those around me!

When you have completed your personal mission statement either frame it and hang it in your office or put it in a place where you can refer to it daily. This is encouragement you need to propel yourself into a quality day with assured positive end results.

Ten Principals and Values for a Successful Life!

1. Today I will begin a new Life! I will shed the old habits and develop new ones that will propel me into the realms of success!

2. I will greet this day with love in my heart for all mankind. I will refrain from judgment and see everyone as a child of God.

3. I will not give up on the brink of a miracle. I will persist until I create a win - win situation.

4. I am God's greatest miracle - one of a kind - unique in many ways. There is a fire within me that will create a positive difference today!

5. I will see today as if it is my last on earth. I will not procrastinate what is to be done today. I will expect success!

6. I will take charge of my emotions. I will use my spiritual power source as the foundation to my actions and allow it to control my emotions.

7. I will choose to laugh much each day regardless of my circumstances. This will support my positive attitude and will instill hope to others.

8. Today I will be like a grain of wheat and multiply my value many times over. I will realize that I must plant my seed in fertile ground in order for this to take place.

9. I will take positive action on all of the above without delay. I know that only when I take positive action will success be mine.

10. I will cry out to God for help. I will pray for guidance and I will listen to God's response and follow His direction's.

HOW TO HAVE A SUCCESSFUL WEEK!

My plan for how I expect every week to go! So many people are into saying TGIF (thank God it is Friday) sending the message that they are glad it is over.

TGIM (THANK GOD IT IS MONDAY) I WILL HAVE A GREAT MONDAY TO BEGIN MY QUEST FOR A GREAT WEEK.

TGIT (THANK GOD IT IS TUESDAY) I WILL HAVE A SUPER TUESDAY BECAUSE I HAD A GREAT MONDAY!

TGIW (THANK GOD IT IS WEDNESDAY) I WILL HAVE A TREMENDOUS WEDNESDAY BECAUSE MONDAY WAS GREAT AND TUESDAY WAS SUPER!

TGIT (THANK GOD IT IS THURSDAY) I WILL HAVE AN INCREDIBLE THURSDAY BECAUSE OF THE GREAT MONDAY, SUPER TUESDAY, AND TREMENDOUS WEDNESDAY!

TGIF (THANK GOD IT IS FRIDAY) I WILL HAVE AN OUT OF SIGHT -TOP OF THE MOUNTAIN - EMPOWERING DAY BECAUSE OF WHAT HAS TAKEN PLACE ON MONDAY, TUESDAY, WEDNESDAY AND THURSDAY!

This of course is all about "ATTITUDE"! I suggest you ask yourself the following question every morning and especially on Monday morning, "ATTITUDE IS CONTAGIOUS - IS MINE WORTH CATCHING?" In other words would you like to meet you? If not go back to bed for five minutes have a conversation with God and realize He is in charge of all problems and He does not need your help!

Place your faith in God and know His word is true for He wants us all to prosper and have a great life. This is not to say there won't be issues, but it is to say He will always lead us through. This is hard to maintain sometimes but it is always worth it!

PAIN IS INEVITABLE! MISERY IS OPTIONAL! Just don't exercise the option!

Now that you have completed this book and it's exercises, remember, your journey is not complete. This journey should go on for the rest of your life. The process of positive growth is a never-ending endeavor. Keep this book handy and refer to it often as you continue your quest for success. Trust in God and seek His face continually for He knows the way.

I truly hope that you have taken the time to digest and discover new ways to approach your life. In addition I hope you have discovered things you used to do and haven't been doing and are now ready to get back to them. We all have a tendency to take short cuts as life unfolds. Short cuts are not always a bad idea, however, many times they diminish the magnitude of the expected results. When we do this long enough we just accept the outcome. So if this book has been a wake up call for you then I am glad for you. Writing it was a big wake up call for me!

It is my ardent hope and prayer that this book has sparked a revival in you so that from this point on you will take the responsibility to become positively different then you were before, expecting more and sharing more. You are the only person living in your body and WHO YOU ARE MAKES A DIFFERENCE! After all, you are worth it!

May your Attitude Always Be Golden
And May your Key open every Door of Opportunity

*Having tremendous success is your birth right.
Getting it is your responsibility!*

The choice is yours, **GO FOR IT!**

www.ingramcontent.com/pod-product-compliance
Lightning Source LLC
Chambersburg PA
CBHW051807040426
42446CB00007B/558